VOICES OF EXPERIENCE

acial Equality · **Judith Rutherford** Chief Executive at Business Link · **Karan Billimoria** Founder of Cobra B
tainment · **Nicola Horlick** 'Supermum' · **Sir John Harvey Jones** Business Leaser · **Tina Knight** TV pres
erton Business and investment writer · **Michael Cole** PR guru · **Bob Bevan** Top after dinner speaker · Ri
ne Novelist and deputy editor of *The New Statesman* · **Debbie Moore** founder of the Pineapple dance stu

Equality · **Judith Rutherford** Chief Executive at Business Link · **Karan Billimoria** Founder of Cobra B
tainment · **Nicola Horlick** 'Supermum' · **Sir John Harvey Jones** Business Leaser · **Tina Knight** TV pres
erton Business and investment writer · **Michael Cole** PR guru · **Bob Bevan** Top after dinner speaker · Ri
ne Novelist and deputy editor of *The New Statesman* · **Debbie Moore** founder of the Pineapple dance stu

Equality · **Judith Rutherford** Chief Executive at Business Link · **Karan Billimoria** Founder of Cobra B
tainment · **Nicola Horlick** 'Supermum' · **Sir John Harvey Jones** Business Leaser · **Tina Knight** TV pres
erton Business and investment writer · **Michael Cole** PR guru · **Bob Bevan** Top after dinner speaker · Ri
ne Novelist and deputy editor of *The New Statesman* · **Debbie Moore** founder of the Pineapple dance stu

Equality · **Judith Rutherford** Chief Executive at Business Link · **Karan Billimoria** Founder of Cobra B
tainment · **Nicola Horlick** 'Supermum' · **Sir John Harvey Jones** Business Leaser · **Tina Knight** TV pres
erton Business and investment writer · **Michael Cole** PR guru · **Bob Bevan** Top after dinner speaker · Ri
ne Novelist and deputy editor of *The New Statesman* · **Debbie Moore** founder of the Pineapple dance stu

Equality · **Judith Rutherford** Chief Executive at Business Link · **Karan Billimoria** Founder of Cobra B
tainment · **Nicola Horlick** 'Supermum' · **Sir John Harvey Jones** Business Leaser · **Tina Knight** TV pres
erton Business and investment writer · **Michael Cole** PR guru · **Bob Bevan** Top after dinner speaker · Ri
ne Novelist and deputy editor of *The New Statesman* · **Debbie Moore** founder of the Pineapple dance stu

Equality · **Judith Rutherford** Chief Executive at Business Link · **Karan Billimoria** Founder of Cobra B
tainment · **Nicola Horlick** 'Supermum' · **Sir John Harvey Jones** Business Leaser · **Tina Knight** TV pres
erton Business and investment writer · **Michael Cole** PR guru · **Bob Bevan** Top after dinner speaker · Ri
ne Novelist and deputy editor of *The New Statesman* · **Debbie Moore** founder of the Pineapple dance stu

Equality · **Judith Rutherford** Chief Executive at Business Link · **Karan Billimoria** Founder of Cobra B
tainment · **Nicola Horlick** 'Supermum' · **Sir John Harvey Jones** Business Leaser · **Tina Knight** TV pres
erton Business and investment writer · **Michael Cole** PR guru · **Bob Bevan** Top after dinner speaker · Ri
ne Novelist and deputy editor of *The New Statesman* · **Debbie Moore** founder of the Pineapple dance stu

Equality · **Judith Rutherford** Chief Executive at Business Link · **Karan Billimoria** Founder of Cobra B
tainment · **Nicola Horlick** 'Supermum' · **Sir John Harvey Jones** Business Leaser · **Tina Knight** TV pres
erton Business and investment writer · **Michael Cole** PR guru · **Bob Bevan** Top after dinner speaker · Ri
ne Novelist and deputy editor of *The New Statesman* · **Debbie Moore** founder of the Pineapple dance stu

Equality · **Judith Rutherford** Chief Executive at Business Link · **Karan Billimoria** Founder of Cobra B
tainment · **Nicola Horlick** 'Supermum' · **Sir John Harvey Jones** Business Leaser · **Tina Knight** TV pres
erton Business and investment writer · **Michael Cole** PR guru · **Bob Bevan** Top after dinner speaker · Ri
ne Novelist and deputy editor of *The New Statesman* · **Debbie Moore** founder of the Pineapple dance stu

Equality · **Judith Rutherford** Chief Executive at Business Link · **Karan Billimoria** Founder of Cobra B
tainment · **Nicola Horlick** 'Supermum' · **Sir John Harvey Jones** Business Leaser · **Tina Knight** TV pres
erton Business and investment writer · **Michael Cole** PR guru · **Bob Bevan** Top after dinner speaker · Ri
ne Novelist and deputy editor of *The New Statesman* · **Debbie Moore** founder of the Pineapple dance stu

VOICES OF EXPERIENCE

THE PROFESSIONAL'S GUIDE TO MAKING GREAT PRESENTATIONS

JACQUI HARPER MBE

EXPERT TIPS FROM HIGH-PROFILE PRESENTERS

howtobooks

Published by How To Books Ltd,
3 Newtec Place, Magdalen Road,
Oxford OX4 1RE, United Kingdom.
Tel: (01865) 793806. Fax: (01865) 248780.
Email: info@howtobooks.co.uk
http://www.howtobooks.co.uk

British Library Cataloguing in Publication Data
A catalogue record for this book is available from the British Library.

Produced for How To Books by Deer Park Productions, Tavistock.
Typeset by Baseline Arts Ltd, Oxford
Cover design by Baseline Arts Ltd, Oxford
Printed and bound by Bell & Bain Ltd, Glasgow

NOTE: The material contained in this book is set out in good faith for general guidance and
no liability can be accepted for loss or expense incurred as a result of relying in prticular
circumstances on statements made in the book. Laws and regulations are complex and
liable to change, and readers should check the current position with the relevant
authorities before making personal arrangements.

Client feedback on Crystal Business Training

"I've been on many courses but nothing has helped as much as this – great to be given things to build on your strengths rather than feel you have to start all over again" – **Senior Manager, Microsoft**

"I now can go into a presentation knowing that I am going to make a good impression" – **Executive, Unilever**

"The training gave me the confidence and skills to do the presentation and really enjoy it." – **Executive, Formula One Management**

"The best course I have been on for a long time. The presenters really know their stuff and I learnt lots! I found the course very relevant, both to my work and to wider life skills." – **Delegate, Foreign and Commonwealth Office**

"A very helpful and useful training day to help maximise the initial impact you have with clients." – **Sales Manager, Merck**

"A very practical course tailored to my needs. The trainers were very good at bringing out the best in me." – **Senior Manager, Sara Lee**

"The course brought home just how important it is to focus on the message and the audience and what I want them to take away! Dreadful that it's taken me so long to realise that!" – **Director, AVIVA plc**

"Excellent course. The trainers made the course very relaxed but very effective & fun. Most importantly I have learnt a lot of new skills to take away and practice." – **Senior Manager, Prudential**

"We now have the confidence and skills to win really big pitches – and we are!" – **Delegate, Business Link**

"They listened, interpreted our ideas and came up with something creative and totally tailored to the needs of my team." – **Abbey Business Manager**

"These special conferences played a very critical role in shaping the effectiveness with which we have been able to execute our change programme." – **Director, ABN AMRO**

"Brilliant understanding of how to work with the media to give the story they want and to get your message across." – **Manager, BT**

"The way Crystal Business Training organised the conferences had a positive influence on the seriousness of these events...it changed the way we work together." – **Board Member, Rabobank International**

"It is the first course that I have been on where I noticed an instant improvement as a result of training." – **Sales Manager, Zurich**

"Excellent session, very focused on my objectives." – **Trainer, First National Bank**

Contents

Preface

This book is dedicated to my husband and children who patiently supported me throughout. For inspiration and so much more I also thank my mother, John Byrne and Brian Collett.

Writing this book has been a brilliant journey for me. It's taken me a little longer than expected (the birth of my son changed the timing by about eighteen months). But three years on I'm still buzzing. I still feel there's a place for a book that gives busy people great ideas and inspiration for their business presentations without long lists of dos and don'ts.

I write this book as a professional presenter. For more than ten years I presented news and current affairs programmes for BBC Television, GMTV and Sky News. I even had my own talk show. I can say without hesitation that my toughest presenting job was fronting the news desk at Sky. Three hours of fast-moving live television filled with interviews ranging from politics to pop music always gave me a huge adrenaline rush. On television, my presentation skills were well developed and operating at full throttle. My tips from the worlds of broadcasting and business are liberally scattered throughout the book.

As a businesswoman I know the value of good presentation skills. It gets you the deal. It gives you status. It gives you profile. I could go on and on. But despite the benefits many people simply dread making presentations.

Dr Desmond Morris, author of *The Naked Ape*, has looked at the psychology of presentation. He believes the fear is rooted in human evolution.

He says, "As the speaker confronts the audience he feels threatened because he is being stared at. The basic reason is that human communication started in small groups of two or three people. Thus, when a man stood in front of a larger group the feeling was unfamiliar, and indeed the others did stare at him."

Thankfully it is possible to get beyond this fear and even enjoy presentations. It requires commitment to get better and access to a variety of techniques to adapt and use as you need them. This book is full of tips to help you do that.

In writing this book I've been guided by my own business experience. As managing director of Crystal Business Training I'm constantly doing presentations: to conference delegates, to clients and to colleagues. I am always looking for new ways to improve my own presentations. I wanted a reference book I could dip in and out of for inspiration and tips. I also wanted to learn from people who excelled in the way they communicated. Hence the creation of this book.

I took a look at great presenters from different fields to see what I could learn from them. For this book I've brought together an eclectic mix of people and each of them have something different to contribute to the science/art of business presentations. Some are business leaders like Sir John Harvey-Jones and Nicola Horlick; some are television presenters like Gary Lineker. You'll also find comedians here including Richard Blackwood. Brain expert Tony Buzan is here alongside PR guru Michael Cole and many others.

I originally intended this book to be a follow-up for delegates on my presentation courses. After the courses I encourage delegates to regularly refresh their presentation style and techniques. I thought that a reference book with lots of ideas and inspirations would help my delegates. As the book got underway it seemed to me that other people might find this book helpful and practical.

So whether or not you've been trained by my organisation, I hope you find among the wealth of viewpoints new insights and tips to enhance your business presentations. All of the interviewees have helped me refresh my own presentations.

I hope you will also find this book fun to read. I've let the personalities of the presenters shine through the text. Learning new information while you're enjoying yourself has always struck me as a powerful combination. I know at school the classes I did well in were always the ones I enjoyed the most. So learn lots, enjoy yourself, give great presentations and maybe I'll interview you for my next book!

Jacqui Harper

Note: Some of the proceeds from this book are going to a charity called Preset which provides leadership skills to inner city youngsters. To find out more about Preset you can visit their website at www.preset.org

Part one Business presentations

Jacqui's tips
- Do your homework
- Look good
- Listen closely
- Be yourself

Business Presentations come in many forms – conferences, pitches, group meetings, one-to-one meetings etc. I can confidently say that I've done plenty well of all of them as MD of Crystal Business Training.

I like doing pitches best because it's like fronting a television programme. First there's the research and editing to get the material into the best shape. Reporting techniques are an engaging way of explaining what you're proposing. Like television, rehearsals are required for pitch meetings. On the big day there's plenty of adrenaline pumping around as you 'perform' your pitch.

I make good use of my television background in other business presentations. Television particularly influences the way I present myself and my message.

In presenting myself I make sure I am always well groomed and well dressed. I tend to go for simpler, understated styles. But I do like a splash of colour somewhere!

I always wear make up to business meetings. I've learnt lots of tricks from the make-up artists who've done my face over the years. The secret of good business make-up seems to be blending it into your skin so there are no harsh lines.

But perhaps the most useful thing television has taught me is the ability to listen well. In television interviews you are always listening to interviewees for nuances and new information. That ability helps me to build rapport with clients quickly and to really understand what they want. I can then tailor my message to what matters to them.

The ability to present is now a fundamental business skill and these days most businesses recognise that. When I train delegates in presentation skills I encourage them to use many of the techniques I used in television news. They're always pleased at how quickly they can increase their impact and confidence.

Sir John Harvey-Jones

Ask businesspeople about Sir John Harvey-Jones and they will immediately think of ICI, the huge chemicals group that he turned around from disaster to prosperity when he was chairman in the 1980s.

Ask people in the street and many will remember Sir John for the Troubleshooter television programmes, in which he showed how to manage a business and nurse it into profitability.

Few will know he was in the Royal Navy from 1937 until 1956, specialising in submarines. After the Second World War he had several intelligence jobs, was seconded to the Cabinet Office and acted as a Russian and German interpreter while Europe was taking shape again.

In 1985 he was awarded the British Institute of Management Gold Medal and the following year the Society of Chemical Industry Centenary Medal.

Sir John now has honorary doctorates from Cambridge, Manchester, Bradford, Leicester, Liverpool and Surrey Universities and is a former chairman of the Wildfowl Trust.

He places great importance on personal contact and face-to-face skills and is understandably busy on the after-dinner speaking circuit. At home you may even find him in the kitchen, as he lists cooking as a recreation in *Who's Who*.

Sir John's interview

The enemy of spin – Sir John Harvey-Jones would not challenge that description of himself. The themes of openness and honesty pervade everything he says about presentation. He even shuns the term self-presentation, making the point that an individual's personality should take a back seat when information is being projected. The facts are important, the individual is a channel.

After almost an entire lifetime in business Sir John has developed finely honed approaches to appearing in front of an audience. His strict view of announcing company results or decisions is that the director in the chair is the chairman of the meeting, not the head of the board.

"You have to go to extreme lengths to ensure that the interests of those at the meeting are met," he says. "You cannot bully them and you cannot be seen to be laying down the law and saying, 'Shut up, listen to this.' An awful lot of people think that in this position they are chairman of the company.

"If the meeting as a whole wants to roast the company, it is important that you maintain a neutral position as chairman of the meeting."

The role alters when the chairman meets analysts or critics. "Then you are speaking as a spokesman for the company," says Sir John. "You must present things fairly and without spin, making the downside as clear as the upside."

Such transparency is important for another vital reason, says Sir John. A bad reputation erodes the company's support in its own community, on which, of course, it depends for a workforce and a good reception for its local policies.

"If there is unpalatable news don't try to obfuscate," he says. "Say it like it is. The people are already expecting far worse than the reality anyway. If a factory has to be shut down it is not their fault. It may be your fault. You cannot pass on the blame to them."

Then comes the particularly important bit: "Show that you care. Communication is actually about emotion, not facts. People remember your demeanour. You must always pick up your own tab. The buck stops with the chairman."

Facing the media has been a regular duty in Sir John's life as a prominent industrialist, one in which a reputation for straightness brings rewards.

"Dishonest men are usually frightened of the press," he observes. "I have always told the truth as I knew it and I recall only once being misrepresented.

"Businessmen don't generally realise what a difficult life media people have, needing to fill up the columns every day and experiencing difficulty in getting the balance right. I have never refused any question from a media person at any time."

Owning up to failings, like giving unwelcome news honestly, is part of the job. Sir John says: "If you have done something wrong be quick to admit it and you get public sympathy. I am a passionate believer in telling the truth to the media – and to the shareholders. More so to the shareholders because they have an absolute right to know everything. You may think their questions are bloody stupid, but remember they are the owners of the company."

For Sir John, pitching for business has always been a positive exercise. "The key thing is always to show what advantages you can offer," he emphasises. "Business is good business only if it is to the benefit of both parties. As an ICI buyer I was taught always to have something on the plate for the other party."

But he warns again against spin and superficial attitudes: "Business is not a one-day wonder. You want relationships with your suppliers. If you screw them, the day will come when they can screw you."

Commercial pitches and information meetings involve another presentation art. How did Sir John handle an audience that might be cynical or in danger of dropping off?

He certainly dislikes aids such as slides and copious handouts. "I think people want to feel they have been spoken to individually," he says. "After all, you know the presentation is being given to a thousand other people too. I always speak from notes. I don't read a speech.

"It is a case of making a bridge with the audience. The presentation I loathe is when you are on a stage and in a spotlight and everybody is blacked out. You need to see people's eyes and notice when they are bored and adjust on the run. Make only three, four or five points and add a little lightness."

Similar presentation rules apply to after-dinner speaking, for which Sir John is now in constant demand. The ideal length of the speech is ten or fifteen minutes – the guests usually cannot take more at such a relaxed event. This means only two or three points can be made. And make 'em laugh for about half of the time.

Sir John is too modest or guarded to single out any of his presentations as huge successes. "It is fatal to say it went well," he says. "You have to be self-critical and scared stiff before you start. The test of when things go well is when things happen as a result. If people go away with a smile you know you have done well."

Does Sir John have any heroes? Two spring to mind. He admires Professor Anthony Clare, the psychiatrist and broadcaster. "He has humour and a deep understanding of the audience," says Sir John. "He can read what is in people's minds very acutely. That is important because the moment you lose the audience it is difficult to get them back."

His other choice is Lord Sheppard, the former chairman of Grand Metropolitan: "He has a good sense of humour, is always in command and is a good listener."

As well as honesty, brevity and humour, are there any special Harvey-Jones tips? Sir John insists that nobody should speak publicly without mugging up on the subject first and paying attention to the art of speaking.

His mind goes back a few years: "When I joined ICI I was given a morning's course on public speaking. It was the most valuable lesson I have ever had. It is such a key part of the businessman's armoury. Anybody who does not consider it is arrogant. He is entering the battle without the weapons."

Sir John's tips

- Show you care
- Limit after dinner speeches to fifteen minutes
- Tell the truth to the media and to shareholders
- In big conferences give the impression you're speaking to individuals
- Get some training in presentation skills

Gary Lineker OBE

Match of the Day presenter Gary Lineker is England's second-highest goal scorer with 48 goals in 80 appearances for his country.

His early broadcasting career included hosting Sunday Sport for BBC Radio Five Live. He joined the BBC's television squad in 1995 appearing on Match of the Day, Sportsnight and Football Focus.

He worked on the BBC's coverage of the 1996 Olympics and presented highlights programmes during Euro 96, and hosted coverage of the 1998 World Cup Finals in France.

He has presented Match of the Day since 1999 and anchored the BBC's coverage of Euro 2000 and the 2002 World Cup.

He had an outstanding football career. He first came to prominence as a forward with Leicester City and had already made his England debut before joining Everton in 1985.

After one successful season (30 goals in 41 games), he was signed by Barcelona and helped them to win the Spanish Championship Cup and the Cup Winners' Cup between 1986 and 1989.

He is well remembered for his Golden Boot-winning performance at the 1986 World Cup Finals in Mexico. At the 1990 World Cup in Italy his goals secured England a place in the semi-finals where they were beaten by Germany in a penalty shoot-out.

Gary retired from international football in 1992. He was made an OBE in 1992.

Gary's interview

You may not think it but making a really good presentation is a lot like doing a penalty shoot out at a top soccer match.

That's the view of ex England soccer captain, Gary Lineker. And he ought to know because he's done both. For eight years he played football at the highest level, scoring 48 goals for England. On television, he's the supercool presenter of Match of the Day, the BBC's flagship football programme.

Today we're used to seeing Gary as the ultimate unflappable presenter – able to cope with all the challenges that live television brings. But it wasn't always so. When Gary ended his football career in Japan in 1994 he was determined to be equally successful at presenting sports programmes. But television was an entirely new game and he had a lot to learn.

Looking back on the early days of his television career Gary admits that it was not easy. He says he wasn't born to present – he's had to learn his craft carefully.

To make things even more difficult he was learning the ropes in front of millions of people when presenting Match of the Day. He recalls that his early presentations were quite wooden, he felt a bit nervous and would occasionally fluff his lines. But crucially says Gary it was not worse than he expected.

The attitude you bring to a presentation, as Gary discovered, is the key to success. Even while developing his skills Gary had a really positive attitude. He admits that his early presenting experiences were tough but he always secretly enjoyed them. The tension and the pressure reminded him of the beautiful game. Gary always felt that a positive attitude would help him succeed.

The hardest thing he had to deal with was the presenter's earpiece. Gary found it tough having a producer talking to him in his earpiece while he was speaking to the audience at the same time. But like many things it got better with practice.

One of the keys to excelling at presenting is speed of delivery, says Gary. Inexperienced presenters frequently make the classic mistake of rushing when they're first sitting in front of an audience. They gallop through interviews and their scripts and the whole thing gets very difficult to manage. "It's really important" says Gary "to take your time and to think about what you're saying."

To be on top of your game as a presenter you also need to be a sharp listener. It's one of the things that separates the skilled presenter from the novice.

He described the hypothetical scenario of somebody interviewing star footballer David Beckham. The last words that Beckham says are "well, I'm going to be retiring next week" and the interviewer follows up with the question "so, who are you going to be playing with next season?". Poor listening skills are one of Gary's pet dislikes.

One of the strategies Gary's developed to avoid this mistake is not writing down interview questions. This encourages him to listen closely to what the interviewee is saying. His preparation for an interview focuses on the subjects to be discussed not the actual questions.

Doesn't he ever dry up using this approach? Gary says occasionally he does forget a question that he had wanted to ask but not very often. He believes it's much more important to turn the interview into an interesting conversation. It needs to feel like a genuine conversation where people are listening and thinking.

He adds, if you worry about drying up it's more likely to happen. If you face the fear and the worst doesn't happen you start to build confidence. Most people surprise themselves and find they can learn to do it well.

Another tip for improving your skills is learning from others. Gary says he had no formal training but he did pick the brains of other great sports presenters like Des Lynam. He also spent time closely watching Des Lynam in the studio.

The key thing he learned from Des Lynam was how to connect to the audience. Part of this is being who you are – being relaxed and natural. It's also essential to include the audience. You can do this subtly with gestures, facial expressions and with a simple smile. There's also inclusive language. You can bring the audience into the programme by saying "joining us in the studio today" rather than "I'm joined in the studio today."

For every presenter dealing with the unexpected can cause the biggest headaches. In Gary's experience "something unexpected often and always happens in television." His advice is to share what's happening with the audience. For example if the autocue breaks down tell the audience what's going on and take a breather to regain composure. "There's nothing worse than a panic-stricken presenter staring into the camera for all their life's worth. It makes the audience feel very uncomfortable," says Gary.

Gary's final tip to presenters is to try to enjoy the experience. Try to look forward to the presentation, to see it as exciting. Remember that you're doing something that some people will never experience in their lives, so it's quite a privilege.

"It's just a great test of yourself. And especially if you do well, it's a great feeling."

Gary's tips

- Show you care
- Have a positive attitude
- Listen closely
- Learn from others
- Accept that things can go wrong
- Enjoy presenting

Nicola Horlick

A bitter dispute in the finance world made Nicola Horlick a household name in 1997 and gained her the title Supermum.

Nicola, born in 1960, studied jurisprudence at Balliol College, but the City, not the law, was to be her line. She joined SG Warburg in 1983 as a graduate trainee and became part of the asset management division. This became Mercury Asset Management and Nicola stayed with it until 1991.

Her steady rise began as she moved to become a director of the UK pension fund business at Morgan Grenfell Asset Management. She was made managing director in 1992 and during the next four years funds under her management quadrupled.

The eruption happened when as a director of Morgan Grenfell she was accused of intending to defect to another institution and to take a team of fund managers with her. She protested that this was never her intention but was suddenly suspended nevertheless.

Nicola flew to Frankfurt to make her protest to the parent Deutsche Bank but it was too late. By this time the media knew her name only too well and 40 journalists had pursued her to Germany.

Nicola then resigned, got out of the limelight for six weeks to write a book, *Can You Really Have It All?*, and joined SG Asset Management, where she remained as chief executive until 2003.

It was during the 1997 acrimony that Nicola was given the Supermum title as a woman flying high in the City and rearing five children. She hates that label, modestly saying that a father in the same position would never be similarly lauded.

Nicola's very human story took a sad turn in 1998 when her eldest child Georgina died from leukaemia. She has since had another child.

The silver lining to the cloud is that Nicola's high profile has enabled her to raise funds galore for Great Ormond Street children's hospital.

Nicola's interview

Everybody remembers Nicola Horlick for a City controversy in 1997. Sadly, that crisis in her life has overshadowed her talents – she is far more interesting to business observers when she is negotiating and presenting.

Her carefully studied approach to meetings is clearly what has helped to make her a winner in the Square Mile. And she says she has got there without ever reading a business book.

That makes sense when she goes on to explain how she handles vital face-to-face encounters. Learning the theory between the covers of a book is little help when you have to think on your feet.

"The key to winning business is to have a good rapport," says Nicola. "The mistake some people make is to go in with a memorised speech. I will not have a prepared script. I have a very strong belief that you must tailor your remarks to the people to whom you are speaking. Nor do I ever have thousands of notes written down."

So in she goes without a well-rehearsed spiel or copious notes but with those indefinable personal skills at her fingertips – and the first is to look straight at your opposite number. "Eye contact is crucial," insists Nicola.

This establishes your confidence but what follows gets the business under way. This is where the thinking on your feet happens. Manoeuvring the conversation to fit the individual is an art that depends on picking up vibes. "You adjust accordingly, having decided whether the atmosphere is formal or informal," says Nicola.

At the same time you must keep remarks brief, she says. "You need to hold people's attention - and their attention span is short." It is interesting that here Nicola says the short attention span is nothing to do with intelligence. Perhaps it has a lot to do with today's business pressures.

"I know that all the people I am dealing with are as good as I am in terms of being professional and being able to do the job." This awareness will act as a brake and keep the interview on the right level.

Nicola emphasises that getting it right first time is a must in the finance sector. "The way our industry operates is to have more meetings after the initial one," she says. "Things have to go well because I shall want to see the people again, and they must want to see me on a regular basis."

There are occasions, of course, when favourable chords will not be struck and the rapport is missing. Regrettably, the battle is often lost when this is the case. Nicola admits: "If the chemistry is wrong, it sometimes just won't work."

She has similar advice about formal presentations to a business audience. In order to convey a message she bears in mind again that the attention span of her listeners is short. "In ten minutes people will get out of it what they want," she says.

An important way of grabbing attention here, however, is to give presentations with a colleague. One presenter can appear to drone on, however interesting the subject, but a change of voice, possibly with a change of pace, can re-stimulate an audience that is in danger of wandering or dropping off.

More than two presenters would overwhelm the audience. She recalls shuddering at seeing six people arrive for a presentation on one occasion. The mob-handed approach is a king-sized turn-off.

Then Nicola reveals an all-important part of her armoury. She recalls that from the age of eight or nine she entered drama competitions. At Oxford University she continued to indulge her passion for drama and later she auditioned for the Royal Academy of Dramatic Art. "Nothing prepares you better for this kind of thing than acting," she says.

Negotiating and presenting are, after all, a form of acting.

Today she uses actors to train her staff, finding them preferable to professional trainers, whom she finds boring and uninspiring. She tells of a senior woman in her organisation who had good relationships with her colleagues but failed to hit it off with people on the outside.

Nicola sent her to a good actor to learn the ropes. He told her to enter a room and say hello ten different ways. The right hello was a confident, friendly one with eye contact established. "You have to pretend that somebody is your new best friend," she says. "You must be relaxed. If you are tense it makes the other person tense."

Nicola admits to being in a better position than most for one particular reason. "I think I have a tremendous advantage because I am female," she says.

The response in these days of political correctness is that being a woman should not matter. Nicola says that when several contenders are pitching for a contract – a process known in the City as the beauty parade – she is often the only woman. And whatever the liberals say, Nicola declares: "Everyone is likely to remember the woman because she is in the minority."

Nicola has strong views on business dress. She advises: "Dress properly and give the right impression. We have dress-down Fridays in my organisation but it does not apply to those seeing clients. It means you are serious if you are dressed smartly. I think it is crucial."

Nicola adds one final thing. She is highly successful in conducting sales pitches and staging business presentations but don't ask her to speak at your company dinner. "I can't do after-dinner speeches," she confesses. "I can't entertain and I can't be witty."

Nicola's tips

- Establish eye contact
- Pick up vibes
- Treat every situation as individual, so ditch prepared speeches
- Be brief
- Dress well

Debbie Moore

The City's abiding memory of Debbie Moore is the sight of her in a short ra-ra skirt standing on the floor of the London Stock Exchange, surrounded by starchy City types. It was November 1982 and Debbie had just taken her Pineapple dance studio business public. Mouths were agape at the first woman allowed to walk on the trading floor.

Her early life was less spectacular. Debbie, the daughter of a plumber and a clerk, was born in Manchester. She left school at 15 and went on a secretarial course. While there she entered a magazine modelling competition and was offered modelling work by Courtaulds at £5,000 a year.

Modelling brought her into contact with Cliff Richard, George Best, David Bailey and others, and she became the face of Revlon.

She started Pineapple as a dance studio in 1979 – in an old pineapple warehouse in London. Soon the business expanded into producing dance wear and three years after formation it went public.

By 1988 Debbie had become worried that the shareholders were too concerned with profit and she bought her company back again.

The main Pineapple studios are now often used for rehearsals by dancers in West End shows and the clothing range sells all over the country.

Debbie says her secret is that she loves every minute of her work.

Debbie's interview

Go in there prepared and positive. The two words encapsulate Debbie Moore's determined attitude when she presents herself at a business meeting.

When you ask Debbie about getting business meetings right she tells you that you must have notes handy. You have to keep glancing discreetly at those notes to keep the talks on track and keep them going your way. "You can do that only if you have thought out what you want to achieve in the meeting," she says.

And that spells preparation. Not only should you get the plan of campaign right, but you should also research the company with which you are negotiating.

So far so good. This is fairly common conventional advice for people who are going into a room to meet their opposite numbers in another company and are hoping to strike a good deal. However, what was a little unfamiliar to Debbie was the business suit, which is still a badge of the City of London.

Debbie's early career had been in modelling. She had been the Revlon girl and had mixed with rock and pop stars and a galaxy of others in the celebrity world. Could she make the giant leap into a business suit?

She felt she had to change the garb to match the job. She did wear a business suit but then came round to thinking she did not have to conform quite so strictly. So on one occasion she went to the London Business School in smart and tasteful non-City clothes and made the point to the students that this was the way – a woman did not necessarily have to be in a business suit. "You just have to be neat and look organised," says Debbie.

To convey this impression to the meeting you have to have everything you need to hand, and this means that tipping out your handbag on the table to find a pen is not an option.

"You must look in control," she says, "even if the kids at home are screaming." She learnt early on that the family back home had to be in good order so as not to interfere with the conduct of business.

Then comes the positive bit. "Obviously, I always talk in a positive and enthusiastic way," says Debbie. "I emphasise that the other people want the brand name we have, and usually they do."

You can walk into the meeting well-prepared, with a positive mind and smartly dressed but you still need an opening. Debbie believes that if you have defined objectives for these talks you should announce them at the outset. If possible, add an ice-breaker. Somebody on the other side may have a familiar face. Your paths may have crossed before. Recall that you met a year ago at the Institute of Directors and the familiar face is likely to respond with a look of recognition.

Debbie says she always tries to bring in the lighter touches, believing that most people, however exalted they are on the corporate ladder, have a human side to them. Most of the sober-sided people in the business world have wives, children, frailties and outside interests, and Debbie finds the best way to oil the wheels is to humanise the whole meeting.

She says she always remembers to keep the process in perspective. "Whatever is being done, it is not a matter of life and death," she says. "It is only a business meeting."

The gravity can be lifted from your mind, but the aim of the meeting is to achieve results, nevertheless. Trickier moments do crop up and these have to be dealt with. So what should you do when difficult questions are thrown at you?

Debbie believes you should confront this kind of problem head-on, even if the question is unanswerable at the time. Honesty is the best policy. You can say: "That is a difficult one. I haven't thought about it." You can tell them: "I hadn't even considered that."

Debbie recalls what an obedient pupil she was at school. She always answered when she was asked a question. When you are uncertain it is better not to hunt hopelessly for a precise answer. A good move can be to ask: "Why are you asking that?" This tosses the ball back into the other side's court with an invitation to give more of an explanation.

The worst thing is to be obviously flummoxed by a poser. "You should not be like a rabbit caught in the headlights," says Debbie.

Even blunders are grist to the Debbie Moore mill. "In all my years in business I have made mistakes and learnt from them," she says. "Mistakes often lead to something better." So don't despair if at one meeting the difficult moment floors you.

Back to the human touch. "Smile at all times," says Debbie. "The deal you are making can be a marriage between two companies and it is meant to keep everybody happy."

Parting shots should be upbeat too. Debbie believes you should sign off with a smile and a promise that you will confirm in writing what has been decided.

Debbie is a champion of the woman in business, so does she think women have an advantage at the negotiating table? She is a little hesitant here but thinks women are regarded as more honest.

"Women don't have as many skulduggery ways of making something happen," she says. "They are more believable."

Perhaps, after all, women have a headstart.

Debbie's tips

- Be prepared
- Be positive
- Be enthusiastic
- Keep the meeting on course
- Keep a sense of humour
- Look organised and in control
- Smile
- Be constructive with the difficult questions
- Learn from your mistakes

Lord Herman Ouseley

Lord Herman Ouseley is Managing Director of Different Realities Partnership which works with a range of organisations on diversity issues. He was previously Executive Chairman and Chief Executive of the Commission for Racial Equality from 1993-2000. Before that he was a local government officer for 30 years, serving as Chief Executive of the London Borough of Lambeth and the former Inner London Education Authority.

He is involved in many organisations on a voluntary basis and is the Chair of three organisations: PRESET Education and Training Trust, Kick-It-Out Plc (Let's Kick Racism Out of Football campaign) and the Policy Research Institute on Ageing & Ethnicity (University of Central England).

He is actively involved in the work of many independent and voluntary organisations including the Institute of Race Relations and the Ethnic Minority Foundation.

He is non-Executive Director of Focus Consultancy Ltd, Brooknight Security Ltd and Quiktrak.

He was knighted in 1997 for services to local government and race equality in the UK, and became a member of the House of Lords in 2001.

He is the current President of the Local Government Association.

Lord Ouseley's interview

Making presentations in difficult circumstances is something Lord Herman Ouseley knows he can do. His toughest challenge occurred when he made a farewell speech for a controversial colleague who was admired and loathed in equal portions by the audience.

Lord Ouseley wasn't phased by the situation because he is a seasoned presenter who's learned strategies that get him through the most difficult situations.

For him the most important thing to do is to prepare well. Lord Ouseley's preparation is thorough but not conventional. He can make up to 300 presentations a year so he chooses not to write down lots of things. His written preparation usually amounts to a few bullet points done on the train on his way to the presentation. Instead he spends most of his time thinking through his presentations.

For the farewell presentation to the controversial colleague Lord Ouseley had lots of scenarios in his mind. Deciding which one to use was a fine balancing act. On the one hand he wanted to get across a powerful message to his internal audience. He was also well aware of the track record of his colleague at the organisation and that there were many working relationships that had broken down with her.

Another aspect of Lord Ouseley's preparation occurs on the day of the presentation. He takes time to read the mood of the audience. He said "some were there to celebrate her departure, some were sad to see her go, some were there for the formality of an evening 'do'. I got a sense of what people wanted to hear and what I wanted to say."

Right up to the moment he started speaking Lord Ouseley was still considering how he was going to weave together his message and how he would end the speech. He was thinking on his feet as he does frequently in the House of Lords. In the highly competitive House he continually comes up with different options and variations of a question to give him a better chance of getting an issue addressed.

Lord Ouseley knew the key to making the farewell speech work was finding a strong start. As glasses clinked and guests mingled the speech suddenly came together for Lord Herman. "I often find if I have the right kick off then the rest flows well" he says.

In this case the right start was tongue-in-cheek. "I think I started with something like 'we're here to see the back of someone who was a thorn in the side of many people!'" said Lord Ouseley. His opening was designed to get attention and to make people wonder where he was going to take the presentation.

In fact he went on to paint a picture of the woman most of the audience recognised. She did not stand fools gladly and no one was spared her bright and abrasive touch, including Lord Ouseley.

He then moved on to the focus of his presentation which was a reflection on why she behaved liked this. His core message was that it takes different styles to take an organisation forward, including hers. The woman's style, despite the accompanying irritation, was useful. It provided the kind of challenge that results in organisational change especially benefitting black employees and women employees. Indeed her strength gave others the inspiration to stand up to powerful people.

The presentation was well received by the audience of 150 people many of whom were local government councillors. This was partly because he mixed humour with serious points. Alongside recollections of Lord Ouseley's struggles as a young black male in South London there were comical descriptions of the power plays in large organisations.

Some of Lord Ouseley's techniques are high risk. In the farewell presentation he used the term 'Black Bastard' – referring to one of the names he was called on the streets of South London. He reduced the phrase to the acronym BB which he also knew were the initials of the departing colleague. Through repetition and humour he managed to transform an offensive phrase into an affectionate reference to his colleague. His risk paid off.

So how did he learn to pull off this kind of presentation? There was no formal training. He does remember being inspired by eloquent and inspirational people early in his career. There are two individuals who were particularly significant.

He mentions the late Rudy Narayan - the black lawyer who was active in civil rights campaigning in the UK. He remembers seeing Rudy at his best: in countless political meetings Rudy's flamboyant and articulate presentation style had people eating out of his hands. Sadly, he says, the talented lawyer lost his way.

The other significant influence was a debater at London's famous Speaker's Corner in Hyde Park. "Some people would describe his speaking as a rant but it was well coordinated" says Lord Ouseley.

In addition to observing good speakers he also consciously makes an effort to improve his speaking skills. After every presentation he reflects on its effectiveness.   He considers whatever mistakes he's made and learns from them. He also listens to feedback.

But after he's delivered a presentation and considered the learning that's it. By the time he leaves the event his mind has already moved on to the next presentation.

Lord Ouseley's tips

- Don't spend time on people you cannot win over at the expense of making your point
- Find your own presenting style
- Take on new challenges to improve your skills
- Use humour when you can
- Listen to feedback – sometimes it's very helpful

Karan Bilimoria

The founder of Cobra Beer was born in Hyderabad in 1961. He gained a commerce degree in India before coming to Britain to pick up more qualifications and become an energetic figure in British business.

Bilimoria became a chartered accountant, obtained a law degree at Cambridge and spent some years with the large accountancy firm Ernst & Young.

He developed the taste for business early. While playing polo as a Cambridge blue in India he thought of starting a polo stick business. There was a British ban on buying polo sticks from Argentina, so Bilimoria imported them from India. His customers included Harrods, Lillywhites and Giddens, the Royal Family's saddlers.

The idea for a lager to accompany Indian food popped up because Bilimoria found English beer did not blend well with the cuisine of the sub-continent and existing lagers were too harsh and gassy.

Cobra is in 90% of the Indian restaurants in the country and there is now a General Bilimoria wine. *Tandoori Magazine* is another of Bilimoria's enterprises – he is the founder and publishing director.

Outside the Cobra business Bilimoria's activities seem full-time in themselves and are too many to list. He is a member of the government's National Employment Panel and chairman of its small business board, and is co-chairman of the Indo-British Partnership.

He is a guest lecturer at Cranfield University School of Management, Cambridge University Business School and the London Business School.

As if all that is not enough, Bilimoria is on the advisory board of a trust that educates the children of poor widows in India and is patron of a mental illness charity.

Karan's interview

Selling is involved in a great deal of human activity, and we often don't realise it. Karan Bilimoria knows all about that, as chief executive of Cobra Beer, a company that must rank as one of the catering trade's greatest triumphs.

Bilimoria rates it highly enough to say: "One of the most important skills in life is the ability to sell."

The importance of selling was thrown into sharp relief for him when he was at university standing in the Cambridge Union elections. Campaigning was a selling job. "We were not allowed to send out leaflets or address big meetings," says Bilimoria. "We went around the colleges and we had to make a sale."

The experience was a valuable introduction to selling, and Bilimoria learnt a basic principle – that the hard work and the striving to convince people had to be preceded by serious preparation.

Some years later Bilimoria was doing the rounds again, but this time he was selling for a living. He started Cobra with a colleague at digs in west London in 1990 and did the rounds of Indian restaurants to sell the lager from a battered old car.

Selling beer to Indian restaurants can be more difficult than it seems. Most of the owners of curry houses are teetotal Muslims and cannot sample alcoholic drinks. So Bilimoria used to leave samples for the restaurants to offer their customers, and his policy usually worked.

The preparation consisted of deciding first what the objective of the exercise was. The aim was obviously to sell the product, so what do you do when the recipient cannot even sip the wares? That is when Bilimoria had to decide he would need to give away a few bottles to clinch sales.

He knew too that the fine art of selling lay to a large extent in listening.

For Bilimoria aggressive tactics were out. Instead, he would want to know what was in his customer's mind.

He had chosen his approach to encourage beer sales in the restaurants where everybody was a non-drinking Muslim, but there would be other forms of resistance.

Money always concerns the customer. "What's the price?" he asks. When he hears the price he may say: "Bring down the price and I'll buy it."

Bilimoria's response: "You have to be able to stick to your price and explain why your product is more expensive. You have to emphasise the benefits. Cobra is smooth and non-gassy. The benefit is that diners can eat more food with it and this means more sales for the restaurant."

It's a good sales pitch but it's also honest and can be delivered in a civilised fashion. The good, straight, reasonable presentation then yields benefits for the salesman. "Customers appreciate integrity," says Bilimoria. "They prefer to buy from people they trust and like."

This reaction is a pleasing one to the salesman who is always thinking ahead to sell some more. You always want to go back and do it again. "Show that you are somebody who is interested in a long-term business relationship," says Bilimoria. "With Cobra we got a re-order rate of almost 100 per cent from day one."

Part of the preparation is deciding what to do when you bash into a brick wall. The salesperson must always be ready to hear no for an answer, but not necessarily accept it.

"If somebody is unreceptive it could be for a variety of reasons," says Bilimoria. "Don't get disheartened because you know he is going to turn you down. This is where being flexible comes in. Listen to him. If you don't know why he is saying no you can't convert the answer into a yes."

The advice is not as obvious as it seems. Some salespeople become irritable or indignant when they are rebuffed. Some become pushy in an ugly way. Others sigh and give up if they fall at the first fence.

The salesperson who understands the reasons for the rejection has the best chance of overcoming the obstacles. The objection could be an irrational one. Perhaps the restaurateur does not want to sell your beer because he has never sold it before. The salesperson can then weigh in with all the benefits to be gained from it.

Bilimoria has a few thoughts on persistence. With so many interests and contacts he is often asked to attend functions and to address organisations. He recalls the man who extended an invitation that he could not accept. He was simply unavailable, not unwilling. The intending host issued three more invitations on dates that the busy Bilimoria could not make.

However, he struck lucky with the fifth invitation and Bilimoria went to the function.

The lesson, he says, is to be persistent but to plug away in a socially acceptable manner.

Then there's the bad news. Every business person has to deal with the unpalatable at some time. Bilimoria's approach, whether in the workplace, in a board meeting or at a shareholders' gathering, is to let people know where they stand.

"You must say whether you are happy or unhappy with something," he says. "Always be open."

Having introduced the problem, however, the bearer of bad news needs to show a positive attitude with a firm statement of what must be done to counter it. "People have to realise leadership is there," says Bilimoria. "At the same time show that you care and understand."

Your plans for a smooth ride at any meeting, however, may be threatened by a one-man awkward squad. Bilimoria's democratic attitude is to let all who attend his meetings have their say, but there can be one difficult customer whose constant questioning is disruptive. What do you do?

Again, Bilimoria suggests building a bridge across to the troublesome questioner. He recommends: "You say that the meeting has a lot of business to get through and that it might be better to discuss the problems being raised afterwards."

It usually works because the questioner is satisfied that grouses will be listened to, and Bilimoria advises: "Try to understand why the questions are being asked."

Is the conciliatory, non-aggressive approach to presentation successful? Bilimoria would no doubt remind you that he supplies more than 5,000 Indian restaurants plus the main supermarkets, and that in most years his company grows by at least 50 per cent.

First principles of presentation in the Bilimoria book:

- Prepare thoroughly
- Listen and understand
- Answer objections constructively
- Establish trust
- Persist

Keith Harris

Keith is currently Executive Chairman of Seymour Pierce. He's held this position since 2003. Previously he was Executive Chairman of IMH plc.

Alongside these roles he's been chairman and non-executive director of a number of media, sport and finance companies.

From 2000 to 2002 he was Chairman of the Football League.

His background in investment banking is extensive. In 1994 he was at HSBC as Chief Executive of one of the largest international investment banks. In 1990 he was Managing Director of Apax Partners Corporate Finance, a boutique style international investment bank. He was also Managing Director and Head of International Investment Banking at Drexel Burnham Lambert Incorporated. He covered all aspects of merger and acquisition advisory and capital markets. He spent seven years at Morgan Grenfell. In 1985 he was President and Managing Director of Morgan Grenfell in New York. In 1980 he was Director of Capital Markets origination and execution for Morgan Grenfell & Co.

He has a first class honours degree and a PhD in Economics.

Keith's interview

In investment banking it's easy to blind people with science but Keith Harris never does. He knows that before you give people detail you've got to engage them and to do that he uses humour whenever he can.

He's had plenty of opportunity to practise his philosophy. As the boss of City of London financiers Seymour Pierce he's regularly presenting to the investment community in the UK.

At the beginning of a presentation Keith typically searches for a line to make his audience laugh, relax and listen. "I can always stand up and say something – it just comes" says Keith.

He recalls a presentation he made in the early days of his stewardship of Seymour Pierce. The venue was Henry VIII's Great Hall at Hampton Court – huge and resplendent with historic tapestries and a spectacular ceiling. Keith started his presentation with the quip "Ladies and Gentlemen thank you for joining me for dinner at my home!" The audience laughed and things proceeded well. It worked.

He works at engaging his audience in a number of other ways. A good example of this was a very different presentation he made as chief executive of Investment Banking for HSBC. This was a tough presentation because it was delivering a radical message about how the business was going forward. There were going to be major changes and staff would be told they would have to re-apply for their jobs.

To make sure the core message was as clear as possible to the audience he thought about the content for a couple of months. He was constantly writing notes and thinking things over. He even found himself jotting down notes in the middle of the night.

He compares this process of preparation for a presentation to that of good stand up comics before a gig. He says that comics have core material that is 60-70% of their act. They focus on refining the delivery of this material until it's near perfect.

Similarly, by the time Keith made the presentation to his HSBC colleagues he was absolutely sure of what he wanted to say to his audience and how he was going to say it. He spoke for nearly two hours without any notes to 400 people and he chose to speak sitting down.

Early in the presentation he sensed the mood of the audience. They were relaxed and listening intently. He used a risqué joke at the beginning to help ease tension. (I'm afraid the joke is a bit too saucy to relate here but it certainly made me laugh!).

Keith's obvious confidence when speaking to audiences is something he's learned from two sources: working in America and attending a training course in presentation skills.

What did he learn from these sources? To listen, look and get the audience comfortable.

On the subject of listening he was told to note the significance of having two ears and one mouth. He was advised to listen and speak in the same ratio. It's something he eagerly embraces "When you're listening you learn. The trick is not to say too much. It's not only manners for people to listen – it gives good information for presenters to latch onto."

The importance of eye contact cannot be emphasised enough. He hates presentations generated from flip charts, slides or scripts where presenters don't look directly at the people they're addressing.

"Engaging eye contact when speaking and looking away when you're thinking is best. If you master that you give a better impression," he says.

But the most important thing he learned was actually a challenge: to make sure you find ways to present information that make people feel comfortable when listening to you. That's the way to get a serious message across.

Keith needed to put all those lessons into action when he became chairman of the Football League in 2000. He was now addressing completely different audiences to the business crowd. The football audiences had people from all different levels of education and social backgrounds.

Getting such audiences to feel comfortable was not easy and he often had to think on his feet.

He remembers making a keynote speech that had been written for him early in his chairmanship. In rehearsal he had a hunch that he would not present it well and he was proved right.

He started the presentation using autocue but decided to abandon the autocue speech half way through. He knew he wasn't reaching his audience so he ad libbed. Things improved considerably after that despite continual attempts by his confused autocue operator to get Keith back to the autocue speech!

Keith's chairmanship of the Football League was during a particularly challenging period. The League was confronting major issues to do with television rights. At the end of his tenure in 2002 Keith produced his most memorable one liner. He said he was "handing the asylum back to the lunatics."

Keith clearly brings a distinctive style of communication to whatever organisation he leads.

Keith's tips

- Make sure you prepare
- Have a maximum of five points
- Start on a high note

Rowland Rivron

Rowland Rivron was destined for entertainment when he was at school. At 14 he played the drums in his school jazz orchestra. At 18, while still at school, he was working as a jazz drummer in the West End of London four nights a week.

He played the drums for the television show The Comic Strip Presents. "All I ever wanted to do was play the drums," he says.

But as he was already in the entertainment world he came to know a lot of people. At one time he and Rik Mayall shared a place when they were both between flats. In his own words he "fell in" with Mayall and Ade Edmondson and wrote comedy material with them.

He followed this by working as part of a band called Raw Sex that appeared on the French and Saunders show, and was then a ragged character called Dr Martin Scrote on Tonight with Jonathan Ross.

Rowland's many appearances on holiday programmes began when he stood in for Caron Keating to present Holiday.

He lives in north London with his family.

Rowland's interview

If you went on the stage during the old music hall days they told you to make 'em laugh. It was great advice for life itself.

For the comedian and musician Rowland Rivron it tops the list. And for one simple reason. "When you have made people laugh you have put them at their ease," he says. Those who cringed when Mrs Merton failed to get a titter out of Chris Ewbank on her television chat show would see vividly what he means.

Humour made everything work for Rowland when he hosted Good Stuff, a television programme about what was happening in London.

"Every week I was chatting to four or five people I had never met before," he recalls. "I found the quickest way of getting round the feeling that these people were strangers was to have a good laugh with them. People drop their guard when you have a genuine laugh with them."

Shared jokes and quips not only strip away any reserve that interview subjects and audiences may have. They also blot out any preconceived ideas they may harbour about you, says Rowland. So often we are wrong to think that a reserved man has no feelings. As soon as a few chuckles have broken the ice he may appear outgoing and amusing too.

There are, of course, many ways of lightening up uneasy and tense moments. Rowland once went with a colleague to do a Virgin Radio interview with the Hollywood actor and dancer Patrick Swayze. The star was in London to promote a new film he had made with Terence Stamp and was probably becoming weary of the obligatory media interviews.

Rowland looked around the hotel room and told Swayze he would only be adding to his boredom by talking to him across a table. "Pretend you are in the shower while being interviewed," Rowland suggested.

Swayze liked the idea and the shower was turned on. The idea worked. On radio the sound of the running water created the illusion that Swayze was actually having a shower as he answered questions and told stories. "It was a good bonding thing," says Rowland.

The unusual laughter-making ruses are Rowland's speciality. "You can ask the same staid old questions if you like, or you can have a lateral way of doing an interview," he says. "But if you do something out of the ordinary people like it because you are probably the 28th interviewer they have seen. You see their eyes light up if you are mucking about and they think this part of the day is actually quite interesting."

The BBC television Holiday programme gave Rowland an opportunity to indulge his preference for this off-centre approach. Often he lands in a wonderful sunny location where holidaymakers are perched on the beach practically naked. "In these shows I have tried to appear at odds with the environment," he says.

Therefore, in temperatures of 90 fahrenheit he slips into a pinstripe suit to speak to men in bathing briefs and women in bikinis. Suddenly the funny man seems like a fish out of water. "This phases people," he grins. "Then they do whatever you say and answer whatever questions you ask them."

Radio, naturally, makes somewhat different demands on the presenter. But triggering laughter is still the principle in a radio studio without an audience. Rowland presents a three-hour Saturday afternoon show on LBC with Janice Vee, the former Link and Bikini pop star. The programme, intended as an irreverent look at life, is called simply Rowland Rivron with Janice Vee.

Rowland says: "If I can make Janice laugh it's like having an audience. There is nothing better than getting someone laughing uncontrollably. But it must never be a private joke, for the listeners' sake."

The same treatment applies to guests on the show. "I can't chat to people for four or five minutes without trying to make them laugh," says Rowland. "That's my litmus test."

He adds a word of caution, however. "You have to be quite astute and read the situation quickly," says Rowland. It is disastrous if the interview subject just does not respond. You spot the problem usually when the first joke misfires and you have to change your approach immediately. Remember Mrs

Merton and Chris Ewbank. Fortunately this was a comedy show but there could have been grave embarrassment in more serious circumstances.

Tailoring the approach to the conditions was never more important than when Rowland hit calamity on one of the Good Stuff television programmes. An unusual aspect of the show was interviews conducted in a limousine driven around London. Rowland's guest on this occasion was the actress Jenny Agutter.

Jenny stepped into the limo with a big smile and put her handbag on the floor of the car, right beside a bottle of sparkling wine.

As the limo moved off the cork popped out of the bottle and the wine poured itself into the actress's handbag. The interview had started with hilarity and fun but very quickly Jenny was hinting: "Can we get this over with as soon as possible?" She was hardly pleased and no jokes would have mended her mood.

All's well that ends well, however. Rowland says: "I have seen her since." And what do they do when they meet up again? "We laugh about it," says Rowland.

Roland's Tips

- Find ways to make your audience laugh
- Think creatively about how to get people to speak to you
- The element of surprise often helps rapport
- Be flexible when things take an unexpected turn
- End early if you need to

Tina Knight

Presentation is a vital part of Tina Knight's life. Her face has been seen on the BBC's Question Time and Breakfast News. She regularly appears as an after-dinner and meetings speaker, and once addressed 3,000 business people at the Institute of Directors' annual conference.

Her fame on the platform preceded her in the business world. From 1985 until 2002 Tina was the owner and managing director of Nighthawk Electronics, a company considered to be a world leader in computer resource sharing devices.

She had started the company with £4,000 and took sales past £2 million in three years. She was regarded as one of the few women to be successful in computers and electronics.

In 1988 she won the Women in Business Award presented by Margaret Thatcher during her time as Prime Minister, and ten years later she received the title of UK Business Pioneer at the Global Summit of Women.

Addressing audiences became second nature and she put this experience into practice by helping to set up the Professional Speakers Association.

She sold Nighthawk Electronics in 2002 but retained a parallel company, Nighthawk Enterprises, based in Saffron Walden, Essex, covering her business training and public speaking activities. At the same time she is a director of J.I.T. International, a non-profit company providing business training for women in Third World countries.

Her charity activities embrace Addenbrooke's Hospital in Cambridgeshire, Feed the Children, Macmillan Cancer Relief and the Cambridge Hospice for Children.

Tina's interview

Start by treating public speaking as an opportunity to share experience with large numbers of people all at the same time. That's what determines the mood for Tina Knight. That's what makes sense for her as a founder of the Professional Speakers Association. And it reinforces a speaker's belief that the members of the audience are there because they want to receive the message.

Tina explains: "I've started and run several businesses in my time and I think people enjoy hearing how I did it first-hand. Certainly I can give them quite a few tips on what makes businesses successful – and what makes them fail.

"Public speaking is also a chance for me to demonstrate to audiences that hard work really does pay. I'm a living example.

"Lastly, audiences seem to enjoy the story of my early entrepreneurial experiences. It's a funny story, though sad in places, and most people find there are lessons to be learnt from it."

Obviously the self-confidence is necessary if the speaker is to put ideas across. The listeners usually pick up the vibes and detect when a speaker is uneasy. It's an uneasiness that makes them feel uneasy.

Tina, however, never takes her audience for granted. Her belief that the people assembled want to hear her is the only assumption she makes. She never assumes anything about their attitudes or interests. "I find out about them," she says, "or at least my researcher does, if I'm too busy."

The conscientiousness stems from respect for an audience. "There's nothing more patronising and annoying than bigwigs who think they can reel off the same old speech, whatever the audience," says Tina. "If people go to the trouble and expense of booking me to speak to them, the least I can do is to study who they are, what they do, what their problems are and what their aspirations are. I hope that what I tell them is therefore as relevant, helpful and entertaining as possible."

Up on the stage her first shot is to get them laughing. Tina believes her listeners respond to a little self-mocking in the comedy spot. A few failings, real or imagined, put the speaker on the same planet as the audience. It's the "one of us" technique. "This always defuses tension and tends to take the wind out of the sceptics' sails," says Tina. "It also helps to show the audience that I'm human with a sense of humour, not some pompous old windbag."

False posturing, however, is not in the book for Tina. A laboured absurd stunt, such as a stage-managed trip over the cables, is just not on. "I try to be myself," she insists. "There's nothing that disarms sceptics faster than total sincerity."

The lighter touch overlays Tina's presentations. She recommends a logically progressed argument but likes to add to it throughout with amusing, but true, stories. "Story-telling as a presentation and training device has become fashionable only recently," she observes, "but I've been telling stories to illustrate my points for years now." Entertaining tales have a freshness that helps to imprint an argument on the listeners' minds.

She comes back then to the principle that you should know your audience before getting jokey. The gags have to be tailored to the audience. For example, the chamber of commerce is usually a different animal from the rugby club. Tina consults a professional comedy writer for some of her material, and she always keeps the party clean. "I never tell any joke that is faintly blue, even after dinner," she says. "Smut is something I just don't think is necessary. There's so much to laugh at around us in the world that isn't smutty. Who needs it?"

Even in the best circles you get the awkward squad or the Mr Smarty who takes pleasure in interrupting, though Tina maintains these people are not as thick on the ground as you might expect. If the disruptive voice does pop up, Tina zooms in and involves the person. She asks for an argument behind the disagreement and shows respect for that opinion. "It's usually enough to defuse any cynicism or anger," she says.

If the nuisance continues, she issues an invitation: "Come and see me afterwards and we can have a chat."

She usually winds up the presentation with a punchline, but never the same one twice. Again, it's horses for courses. Arguments and points emerge unexpectedly and unannounced during the presentation and these may determine how the big finish goes.

Tina recalls: "On one occasion I was speaking at a venue within a large complex, and unbeknown to the organisers of my event the complex managers had decided to test the fire safety equipment that day. My speech kept on being interrupted by a voice on the tannoy asking everyone to evacuate the building, followed by another one saying that this was just a test and should be ignored.

"My punchline that day was something like, 'I hope you enjoyed the suspense and excitement I arranged for you by keeping you guessing whether or not the building was on fire.' That got a huge laugh." It is a perfect example of using a situation.

The duration of a speech is equally important to Tina. She uses a well-worn comparison: "A speech is like a woman's skirt – short enough to be interesting, but long enough to cover the subject matter."

She says she aims at keeping the formal part of a presentation as brief as possible and then engages the audience in a question and answer session. Here she has further thoughts on interjections during a speech. The interruption, though taken seriously, should not develop into a question and answer interlude. This can halt the flow of an argument and introduce topics that were due to come up later anyway. There's no point in messing up the sequence. The real time for questions, awkward or not, is afterwards.

With a larger audience discussions without a roving microphone are difficult because participants cannot hear one another. The one-to-one interplay in which a question is asked and then answered is preferable.

Discussions come into their own in small groups. Tina says modestly: "I learn as much from them as the audience learns from me. It's useful and people value the fact that you're interested in their views."

A few of Tina's tips

- Share experience with your listeners
- Research your audience and get to know what they want
- Make 'em laugh at the outset
- Illustrate points with stories, particularly funny ones
- Confront the hecklers and quickly answer their objections
- Keep the presentation short and ask for questions at the end
- Send them away laughing

Stephanie Manuel

Everybody remembers Jamie Bell as the dancing hero of the film *Billy Elliot*, which picked up award after award in 2000. Jamie was a student at the Stagecoach Theatre Arts School in Yarm, North Yorkshire, when he was spotted and singled out by the principal for the part of Billy. The film-makers agreed and Jamie became a star.

The Yarm school was one of many acting, singing and dancing establishments in the Stagecoach Theatre Arts Schools that Stephanie Manuel co-founded in 1988 with David Sprigg, a former lending manager with Barclays Bank.

The company, based in Surrey, just went from strength to strength as more schools were opened. In 2001 when the company needed to raise £4 million for expansion it floated on the Alternative Investment Market. By 2004 there were 420 schools in the UK and more than 500 worldwide.

At the time of the flotation Stephanie said of the investment potential: "We are a little different and I think we stand a good chance."

Stephanie Manuel and David Sprigg were still at the helm in 2004, as joint chief executives.

Stephanie's interview

The speaker who has a passion for a subject usually wins the vote of the audience. Stephanie Manuel has that passion.

As the woman who has given her all to the Stagecoach theatre schools, she is mustard keen to tell people how she built up the company and is equally keen to communicate that enthusiasm.

"I talk in public about my business, and for me the key to expression is the passion I have for it," she says. "It is always good for me to talk from the heart. For example, I often make copious notes for a speech. Usually I get through the first two or three sentences and then throw away the notes. As long as I have the good old adrenaline rush I almost always manage to drive the points home."

The passion, then, overrides even the planning. And with the passion comes a close relationship with the audience. Stephanie does it by sharing her feelings. "I believe it is good to take people into your confidence, even a big group, and not to be afraid of showing your true self," she says. "Show them you are human."

This approach has another benefit for Stephanie. It reveals a vulnerability that endears the speaker to the listeners. "I lay myself a tiny bit open," she says.

In some circumstances this even convinces the listeners they have the advantage. Stephanie explains: "If I am addressing people who are better at something than I am, people such as teachers, I say I cannot believe I am speaking to such experts in the field. It says, 'I am nervous but I am giving you my best.' It makes me feel better and it invites people to listen to me on the same level."

The vulnerability is uncomfortably real for Stephanie. She says: "Contrary to expectation, people who speak publicly are not always terribly confident. I stand up with trembling knees – maybe that is what gives one the edge. But I often wish the building where I am going to appear will burn down so that I don't have to speak."

Having started with a little self-deprecation, whether spoken or unspoken, Stephanie uses one or two techniques that clearly betray her theatrical experience. Speakers should never be too quick in their delivery, she says. The machine-gun attack is a brutal deterrent. There is room, too, for the odd pause, to help people to take in what is being said to them.

Like many speakers, Stephanie prefers to get away from all the dull theory and to liven up the points of an argument with relevant stories. They throw the argument into relief.

However, the speaking techniques, all valid and textbook, are useless unless they promote the message, and here Stephanie's vital ingredient is the passion. She puts it this way: "My success depends on whether I am shining through."

Again like many speakers, she appreciates the value of going out on a memorable note, but she admits: "Finishing is quite difficult."

She does not have a set way of winding up a presentation, partly because it is impossible to predict how things will go in the first place. No two audiences are the same. Some can be staid and appear unresponsive and others can be infected by the speaker's enthusiasm.

Throughout the presentation the good speaker tunes in and assesses the mood of the audience. "You play it by ear and you get to know whether the audience is on your side or not," she says.

The address and the finish are to a degree dictated by the audience mood but Stephanie favours ending with a summary of what has gone before. One way of summing up is to go back to the beginning, where usually the whole point of the address is stated. The argument can then be summarised with reference to the aims originally stated and the audience can decide whether the message has come across.

How do you deal with the difficult customer? Stephanie favours a session of questions and answers after the address – and that is when she encounters and replies to the awkward ones.

"I throw the session open to questions from the floor and I quite like it," she says. This is interesting because it chimes with Stephanie's preference for speaking from the heart. When there are questions the speaker is no longer in the driving seat and has to respond from that reservoir of knowledge and experience – and with that all-important passion.

Questions may be awkward but with the adrenaline still pumping Stephanie clearly enjoys a healthy cut and thrust. Essentially, it represents engagement with the audience, which she always wants, but this must not be confused with the angry battering that some groups can dish out. Fortunately, that hostility has not come Stephanie's way.

She says with some relief: "I have never been heckled. I would be mortified if it happened. So I could never be a politician."

Stephanie's tips

- Show that you have a passion for the subject
- Take people into your confidence and show some human weaknesses
- Use stories to illustrate points
- Finish with a summing-up if possible
- Always take questions at the end

Beverly Malone

Beverly Malone brought an impressive pedigree to the job of General Secretary of the Royal College of Nursing, the British nurses' professional union.

For the year before she took up the post she had had the ear of President Bill Clinton. It was her only job that was not strictly in nursing.

Beverly, from Kentucky, gained a nursing degree from Cincinnati University in 1970. Eleven years later she received a doctorate in clinical psychology. Her experience has been wide. She has worked as a surgical staff nurse, a clinical nurse specialist, a director of nursing and an assistant administrator of nursing. From 1996 to 2000 she was President of the American Nurses' Association, which the RCN probably saw as her main qualification for the British job.

Her White House experience followed when she was appointed Deputy Assistant Secretary at the health department, advising on policy and programme development.

Her appointment to the British post in June 2001 had been preceded with a little controversy. Some thought a home-grown candidate should have the job and were worried that Beverly might not easily understand the workings of the British health system. She appears to have been robust enough to weather that particular storm.

A few of Beverly's choice sayings were published when she was up for the RCN job, giving some insight into her character. She said of being a nurses' leader: "My job is to offer my vision. The beautiful thing about it is that when you share the vision it changes. If you hold on to it, it won't change. It will only be your personal vision. The way to make it real is to share it."

Her thoughts on nurses, doctors and power: "We need nurses who have power, and nurses have a lot of power, but we just don't acknowledge it. We don't admit it. It's as if we had it and we left it somewhere. Or we think the physicians are going to figure out that we need it and they're going to just walk up and say, 'I know you have been wanting my power base for a long time. I came to just drop it off for you.' That really is hallucinating, colleagues."

Emotions? She says: "If you have a tendency to cry, don't worry about it. You can get through anything. Just get yourself lots of Kleenex. It shouldn't stop you from accomplishing anything."

Beverly's interview

Telling a good story always goes down well. The stand-up comic knows the value of that device. Remember the trademark phrase of the veteran comedian Max Bygraves. "I wanna tell you a story," he would say, and his fans would salivate with the expectation of a tasty one.

Storytelling is a favourite technique of Beverly Malone, who became General Secretary of the Royal College of Nursing in 2001.

Her job involves addressing the wider health community, nurses and others. She also has to talk tough to government negotiators when the dreaded pay talks come round. Knowing she has to get a vital message across as the representative of thousands of British nurses, she marshals her information carefully before thinking about what stories she has to relate.

"There is some information that you want to state in five or ten different ways as it has to be reinforced during the presentation," she says. And one of those ways could be a story that makes a point in the presentation relevant to the audience.

The telling of stories is something that comes naturally to Beverly. She grew up with it in the United States in Kentucky. For people in the Appalachian hills of Kentucky it was almost a way of life, and Beverly was imbued with it.

The skill has transferred well into the profession that Beverly chose. Nursing is bristling with human stories, some funny, some sad, thanks to the close contact that nurses have with people of all kinds, often in their rawest state. A hospital patient is frequently stripped down emotionally as well as physically.

Beverly says: "There are stories about patients who have made a difference in your life and stories about the way nurses work with one another and how they hold things together for the sake of the patient."

To this great resource Beverly adds tales she collected in her American homeland. One story she tells has the ring of tradition about it and comes straight from the Appalachians.

The story is set in the hills, where a woman is out walking. The woman, who happens to be a nurse, sees what she thinks is a stick lying in the middle of the road ahead. However, as she gets nearer she sees it is a snake. The poor thing is frozen solid because the weather is so cold.

As a nurse whose mission in life is to aid the healing process she takes the snake to her bosom and heads back. At home she takes the snake out and finds it is thawed. But the snake has a lethal sting and it sinks its fangs into her.

As the nurse breathes her last she asks the snake why it bit her. "You knew I was a snake when you picked me up," replies the ungrateful creature.

The point, says Beverly, is that nurses must never think of themselves as victims. In a hospital the nurse is often undervalued in the chain of treating the patient, yet she is the glue holding it together. "Nevertheless, don't play the victim," says Beverly.

One of her tricks of the presentation trade is to call for volunteers to join her on the stage. Nothing works better than live illustrations in driving a point home. One absolute must, of course, is to make the volunteers feel appreciated, so she invites the audience to give them a round of applause.

In one scenario she has a male and a female on the stage. She asks the female to stand as close as she can to the male while still feeling comfortable about it. "But they freak when I try to get them to move even closer," she says.

The point? At work people must know their boundaries. It's part of good organisation, and people don't like you to trespass on their territory.

Often the harder part of the job for Beverly as general secretary of the nurses' organisation is dealing with health authority representatives and civil servants. She tells fewer stories in these circumstances.

Yet stories there are, though not the belly-laugh type. Beverly's approach is to relate everything to patient care. So any tale told has to illustrate vividly the important – and sometimes difficult – part played by nurses in the National Health Service. It should hit home if the people with the purse strings appreciate that it is the patient who matters in the end.

In a high-powered, high-profile job there are bound to be some barbs. How does Beverly present herself when criticism is being aimed at her or her organisation?

"I ask what part belongs to me," she says. She believes there is always some truth in a criticism when somebody goes on the offensive. To react immediately with a blazing gun is never right. To listen to the case always is.

If any of the accusations are just, Beverly says you have to own up. "Then I say, 'This is what we are going to do about it'."

The negotiating and dealing with sticky moments are surely the difficult parts of the job. And certainly Beverly sounds enthusiastic when she talks about addressing an audience as a two-way experience.

"As I speak I try to get the audience to think with me and to anticipate where I am going," she says. "And your presentation must leave people feeling moved and touched by what you have said."

That's the real point.

Beverly's treatment plan

- If something is important, say it several times but in different ways
- Illustrate points with stories
- Involve one or two members of the audience if this helps to emphasise points
- Get your listeners to think with you
- Deal honestly with criticism

Judith Rutherford

Judith Rutherford has been Chief Executive at Business Link for London since 2001. Business Link for London provides business advice and support services to the capital's 332,000 businesses. The company has a turnover of c.£40 million per annum, 370 staff and is principally funded by the Small Business Service.

She led the merger of the nine smaller Business Link companies to establish the current single London-wide company.

Judith is experienced in working at the interface of the public and private sectors. She was Chief Executive at the London TEC Council (1996 – 2000). At this post she led the development of strategy for business support and skills for the London Development Partnership.

Judith has also worked at English Heritage (1995 – 1996). She founded and led AZTEC (1989 – 1995) – one of London's Training and Enterprise Councils. She also worked at the Department of Employment.

Judith's interview

Think pictures. That's the advice from the boss at London's top company for growing small businesses.

As chief executive of Business Link for London, Judith Rutherford regularly speaks to her team of 400 people at staff conferences. At these events her presentation skills are truly tested. Her staff can be critical and exacting.

It was at one such conference that Judith successfully used two pictures to deliver her message. She was outlining the new strategy and wanted to let staff know why changes were being made and the key challenge for the business.

At the start of her presentation up popped the first picture – a slide of the Sistine Chapel by Michelangelo. Eyes were dazzled by the famous 16th century ceiling fresco that lavishly depicts the creation of the world in nine compositions. Although immensely talented Michelangelo struggled to complete his masterpiece because he was juggling the demands of his patrons.

It was a creative way for Judith to get into a discussion about the tensions that occur when meeting the needs of different funders. She proceeded to describe what various funders wanted from Business Link and what actions staff needed to do to meet those requirements – including strategic action.

The second breathtaking picture shown to staff was a slide of the mighty Mount Everest in all its glory. At 29,000 feet it's the highest mountain in the world and one of the toughest challenges for even the most skilled climber.

Formidable too was the target presented to Business Link staff. They were informed that their goal was to serve 100,000 businesses in the capital by 2006. By using the metaphor of climbing Mount Everest Judith was clearly indicating how difficult staff would find this target and was immediately acknowledging the deep scepticism that many people must have felt.

She had tough messages to share with her audience. She approached this with openness and concentrated on explaining why this was the best option for the business. It was important to her that her audience also knew the benefits that would result.

She clearly did get her message across because the feedback from the audience was good. They gave her high scores for fully understanding her message and the use of analogies.

This presentation was a radical departure from Judith's usual presentations. In the past she has used many slides with lots of data. This time the only visuals she used were the two pictures.

Her presentation was distilled to just a few key points. "Boil it down to the simplest messages you can" she says "the audience cannot remember loads of information."

Judith was also trying out new ways of preparing her presentation. She didn't write everything out – she used notes to sound more relaxed and natural. She rehearsed only two times and took ten days to prepare the whole presentation. She also made a deliberate decision not to stay at the lectern.

Apart from staff conferences, Judith regularly speaks to diverse external audiences across the capital – anything from community groups to top government officials. She always works hard at improving her presentation skills. Whenever she's had critical feedback she's taken it on the chin and used it as an opportunity to improve her performance the next time.

Her interest in presenting goes back to schooldays. She remembers enjoying drama lessons and reading out items at school assembly.

Does she still get nervous when presenting? "Oh, yes" she says, "I do try to concentrate on thinking positively. I remind myself how much I want to talk to this audience - and take deep breaths."

Judith says a key thing for any business presenter is flexibility – being able to respond to the unexpected. She gave an example of an event she attended where just about everything that could go wrong did. The delegates were evacuated twice, canapés and drinks were moved at the last minute, the anti-fire sprinklers were activated and the microphones didn't work. She opened her presentation with the words "I'm never going to forget this evening!" and got thunderous applause.

Every presenter at some stage has to work out how to bring an audience back on board. Judith faced this situation when she followed a speaker who spoke too softly. The audience was drifting because they couldn't hear the presenter. So when Judith got on stage she went for it big. That is, she started her presentation with a big, booming voice – and it worked. She was able to get the attention of her audience and get on with her presentation.

And finally, when it's all over the big question facing every presenter is how to do well the next time. It's a question that Judith knows she'll always find an answer to.

Judith's tips

- Wear your best suit for presenting – the audience deserves it
- Adapt your presentation when it matters
- Stick to the bare bones
- Have the confidence to pause

Dame Jocelyn Barrow

Dame Jocelyn Barrow is a Principal Consultant at Focus Consultancy Ltd. She is a senior executive with a distinguished and wide-ranging career in education, public service, and community relations. She has held government appointments with a variety of national organisations, statutory bodies and inquiries. She was a founding member and General Secretary of CARD (Campaign Against Racial Discrimination), which was responsible for developing the Race Relations legislation of 1968.

She has been a senior teacher in Tower Hamlets and later a teacher-trainer at Furzedown College and lecturer at the Institute of Education, London University in the 1960s. She was a pioneer in introducing multi-cultural education addressing the needs of the various ethnic groups in the UK. She was the first black woman Governor of the BBC, and was the first Deputy Chair of the Broadcasting Standards Council.

Dame Jocelyn has been active in voluntary and community organisations for over 35 years, which has included dealing with issues relating to race, gender, women and housing.

In 1972, Jocelyn Barrow was awarded the Order of the British Empire (OBE) for work in the field of education and community relations. In 1992, she was made a Dame of the British Empire (DBE) for her work in broadcasting and contribution to the work of the European Union as a Member of the Social and Economic Committee, representing the UK in Brussels.

Dame Jocelyn's interview

Buckingham Palace acknowledged Dame Jocelyn Barrow as one of the UK's top women achievers at a special luncheon in 2004. Her achievements are in the fields of education, race relations and broadcasting and include being the first black woman Governor of the BBC in 1981.

As a businesswoman Dame Jocelyn Barrow often uses her experience in these different fields to win contracts for Focus Consultancy, a company that pioneered diversity training in the UK.

As a director she has presented winning pitches for contracts worth hundreds of thousands of pounds. She puts her success down to detailed preparation.

One major contract she won involved doing an extensive feasibility study and a pitch presentation. The preparation of the feasibility document involved organising community meetings to persuade ethnic groups of the benefits of the proposed projects.

Rehearsal of the presentation was done beforehand. Three people were involved so "each presenter went through what they were going to say, brainstorming questions and making sure everyone in the team was singing from the same hymn sheet." They also agreed who would answer which questions.

At the rehearsal they calculated that each presenter would have ten minutes to explain their part of the story. The presenters each focused on different subjects. Dame Jocelyn's role was to explain what was achieved in the feasibility study and what it meant for delivering the three-year project.

She used a few slides with bullet points to focus the minds of the panel on the subject. Limiting the number of slides was deliberate because you can "overburden people with too much detail – you need to judge this accurately.

Short, sharp information well presented and well researched is the goal" she says.

The impression Dame Jocelyn Barrow wanted to give the panel at the presentation was that the speakers had a lot more detailed knowledge and expertise to give.

However Dame Jocelyn Barrow has another reason for limiting how much information you give in a pitch presentation. As a consultant she cautions that it is a "disadvantage to put all your ideas on display and so make them public." In her experience organisations can give your information to other contractors who win the contract.

"It can happen to anyone in the consultancy business so it's wise not to give too much away in presentations." She recommends protecting your ideas by publishing articles which demonstrate your expertise. This helps give you ownership of your ideas.

Image was also considered before the presentation. She always makes the effort to go well dressed for a presentation and prefers the overall look to be understated. The point is for your image to exude confidence in yourself and your subject.

She winces as she recalls a recent presentation made to her by two women. The eye make up of the women was over done, especially the use of deep purple eye shadow. "What they said was good but the make up distracted attention and so they lost the pitch" she warns.

Despite the rigorous preparation made by Dame Jocelyn Barrow and her team things did not go to plan at the presentation. First off the presentation team were kept waiting for ages in the corridor. Once the presentation was made the questions asked by the panel were surprisingly simplistic, almost to the point of annoyance. The questioners did not seem to recognise the collaboration done beforehand between themselves and the presenters during the course of the feasibility exercise.

To handle the situation Dame Jocelyn Barrow drew on her experience as a political campaigner on race and gender issues. When campaigning she was constantly judging people's reactions, assessing who was on board and who wasn't. She also learnt that to persuade people you need to give them room to manoeuvre, to change their mind and to reflect.

Dame Jocelyn Barrow soon worked out that the panel had not read the detailed feasibility document given to them before the presentation. She therefore created opportunities for the panel to learn fundamental information about the document. This was done with bridging techniques. She would acknowledge and address their questions and then direct her answer to additional information she felt they needed to know.

The manner in which this was done was crucial. She wanted the panel to feel in control so their questions were always addressed seriously however much she was biting her tongue.

She never directly mentioned the panel's lack of familiarity with the document. To do so would be to endanger the delicate game of diplomacy taking place. Direct comments would indicate that the panel was no longer in charge and had weaknesses. Dame Jocelyn considers it a far better strategy to play to the strengths of the panel.

These tactics eventually paid off. Shortly after the presentation Dame Jocelyn and the team were awarded the contract.

Dame Jocelyn's tips

- Go well dressed
- Focus on the strengths of the panel
- Use the internet to get information about the company and the panel
- Use strategic pauses to keep them with you and to breathe!
- Never get angry – it weakens you

Cristina Odone

To many Cristina Odone is that Catholic woman who makes regular appearances on television. The image can work against her because of the hostility or cynicism with which people with firm views are regarded.

Her chosen career is journalism, and, like most journalists, she wants to be seen as human, with human feelings and human faults.

Cristina was born in 1960. Her father was Italian, her mother Swedish. She studied at Oxford and became a freelance journalist after her degree. She was with *The Catholic Herald* in 1985 and 1986 and then had a brief spell as a diary writer on *The Times*.

She spent four years in the United States but then came the job that gave her the Catholic stamp. For four years she was the editor of *The Catholic Herald*.

In 1996 Cristina wrote her first novel, *The Shrine*. A second novel, *A Perfect Wife*, came out the following year.

She resigned from her job at *The New Statesman* to concentrate on other interests. She has appeared on the BBC programme Question Time.

Cristina's interview

The emotional appeal comes first for Cristina Odone. It's what prepares the ground whenever she has to put a message across to an audience. Emotions determine how people react and receive a message. They are a natural starting point.

They are of particular importance to Cristina because of the message that she regularly carries. When she stands in front of an audience the things she has to say are sometimes unpopular and subject to ridicule.

Unashamedly she declares: "It has been a professional challenge to me to get the Christian and Catholic Church message across to a sceptical or contemptuous audience." And this is where the first emotional weapon is used.

"The first thing to recognise," she says, "is that you can speak to others only if you have a common link. So you appeal to their emotions, you have to play on the likeness between you and the audience. They may come to you with lots of prejudices, but once you have divested yourself of your religious or professional persona and shown them your human side, you have already built a bridge."

As an aside Cristina relates an experience that underlined a prevailing hostility to Catholics. She recalls: "I told the anecdote when I spoke to a Christian audience at Lambeth Palace. When I first went to *The New Statesman* I was asked whether I could work with atheists. I said I could. However, what I was really being told was that colleagues might make fun of me because of my Catholicism."

The human failings that a speaker exhibits are seen by Cristina as a vital part of the bridge-building approach. Not only is the Catholic faith the target for criticism and barbs, but Cristina says many non-believers regard Catholics as self-righteous. "Therefore, don't get on your high horse," she says. She advises that it is better to view yourself as an imperfect human being. When listeners realise the speaker has flaws too, they start to feel warmer inside. The construction of the bridge is well under way. Something in common is being established.

The process involves not assuming any common background. Cristina says: "Whether you are writing or speaking to an audience, it is important to appreciate that what you take for granted is not part of the everyday language of the people you are addressing. At the risk of sounding like a back-to-basics person, you have to strip your ideas down to the most simple common denominator."

There is nothing more irritating than a speaker spouting jargon and assuming that others share the knowledge. Keeping the address simple and comprehensible is a must.

Every speaker, of course, has an individual way of starting a presentation. "You can only grab people with provocation. You have to excite them," says Cristina. "In fact, you have to kick off with a surprise."

She does not share the view of many speakers that a speech has to start with a joke. She illustrates her technique by describing how she opened an article she wrote for *The Guardian*.

"I had to bring people on my voyage and say why the chattering classes hate Christians. I knew I had to come up with a shocker. I was as bold as I could be. I said they hated Christians because they are fearful of them. They are scared because Christians have what they want, the key to happiness."

However, there is more to good presentation than grabbing the audience's attention at the outset and beckoning them over to your side. Even if the listeners don't agree with your argument, you have to keep them interested in it. And you don't achieve that with bland theory. Avoid abstractions, says Cristina. Tell them stories from your experience to bring the argument to life.

Many audiences have difficult customers, as Cristina has found. One example springs quickly to mind: "I had people pelting me with tomatoes once when I was speaking in Ireland. I was quite frightened, but I felt so beleaguered and embattled that I gained strength from it."

These are the circumstances in which the speaker's mettle is tested. The speaker has to stay cool and dignified. "There must be no snide put-downs," says Cristina. Heckling is best taken as a challenge to which the speaker must rise.

Cristina tries to end on a note that sends people away with something to remember. She comes back to the emotional links that she works hard to establish with the audience. She says: "I am an emotional person and, though this may seem like a cheap trick, if you can land an emotional punch and reach out into an emotional area, you should."

She has one reservation, particularly for women speakers. A member of the audience can ask questions or throw criticisms that cannot be dealt with in detail in the course of the presentation. Some speakers invite the questioner to discuss points afterwards, but Cristina urges caution. "There are some people who want to get too close to you, especially if you have a public profile. And this situation is a little more difficult for women."

Cristina's step-by-step guide

- Appeal to people's emotions to create common ground
- Give them an early surprise
- Illustrate points with stories – don't just put dry arguments
- Handle interruptions with dignity
- Finish on an emotional note to maintain interest to the end

Rutger Schellens

Rutger is based in the Netherlands at the Head Office of Rabobank in Utrecht. He is a frequent flyer around the world because of his job as Global Head of Financial Markets and Member of the Managing Board of Rabobank.

Before this Rutger had a successful career with another leading Dutch Bank, ABN AMRO. There he was also immersed in the world of global financial markets. He held a number of positions including Managing Director and Global Head of Corporate Distribution and Managing Director and Global Head of Treasury Sales.

He is a firm believer in developing talent through mentoring and in 1997 he took on the role of coordinator for the mentoring programme for Global Financial Markets at ABN AMRO.

In his early years at ABN Bank he held a variety of roles culminating in the leadership of a team that was active in market-making in European government bonds, global Eurobonds and sales for those products to the Asian institutional investor base. He did this shortly after the integration of ABN Bank and AMRO Bank.

He trained for his career in Amsterdam where he studied for a BA in Marketing and Economics.

Rutger is a member of the board of ISMA – the self-regulatory organization and trade association for the international securities market. He has previously been a member of the conference board of the European Council on Treasury Management. In 1999 he had an active role on the editorial panel of *Treasury Management International* magazine.

Rutger's interview

Rutger Schellens learnt his most important lesson about business presentations from his time as a hockey coach. When communicating tactics and strategy to his young players he quickly realised that short, focused messages got the best results.

So he's taken that winning formula into the highly competitive world of international financial markets. As the head of global financial markets for one of the top Dutch banks, he regularly uses his coaching techniques when addressing international audiences, clients and colleagues.

Rutger recalls a presentation he did to his international team. The global audience of 200 people had gathered to hear the new business strategy.

Rutger's presentation was less than 15 minutes long so it was certainly short. It contained three core messages and he was careful to reinforce them several times.

What did he do beforehand? First of all he made time for preparation in his busy schedule. He spent a day and a half working on the presentation and rehearsing the material with conference producers.

He worked hard at extracting the main messages from his material. He established three core messages which described three initiatives. He made sure that throughout his presentation he constantly went back to those core messages.

He also thought about the best way to start his presentation. After a number of ideas he settled for a video. In this case it was a short television commercial about Rabobank's wholesale division. It took one minute to play the humorous commercial but the laughter and goodwill lasted much longer.

The video was an ice breaker but its theme clearly connected to the core message. The central character in the video is making a presentation to an international financial audience and gets off to a difficult start. But he gradually grows in stature and by the end he is taken very seriously by his audience. This was a fitting allegory for the story of the global bank and a strong start to a presentation explaining how the strategy will fulfil the bank's aspirations.

Half way through the presentation Rutger showed another very short video. It showed him questioning a senior figure in the bank about a key issue which was causing problems to his division. The video explained new practices which tied into Rutger's core message about the way forward. The video was another way of reinforcing the core messages to his audience.

Four slides were created for the presentation. Yes, four. In Rutger's experience this is where many business presenters go wrong. They use far too many slides and put too much information on them.

"You have to be very selective with what you use in a presentation. When talking about results give the audience headline numbers, probably four is the maximum. If you're talking about strategy limit the number of key performers or indicators that you discuss. Also make sure people can see the numbers at the back!"

Once you've got the message clear it's also important to work on delivery, says Rutger. For the strategy presentation he paid attention to pace. He didn't want key points to get lost so he used deliberate pauses. For example when he played the funny video at the beginning he waited until the audience was quiet again and he had their full attention before resuming his speech.

Rutger feels that getting the delivery right helps you reach your audience. He also pays close attention to what he wears. For the strategy presentation he wore a smart dark suit and shirt but no tie. He wanted to show that he was relaxed in himself and with his subject. He also made the effort to smile and articulate his words.

The benefit of working on delivery is that it brings out the presenter's personality. Rutger admires colleagues whose delivery gives the audience the sense that they are being themselves.

A strong delivery is best achieved through rehearsal. "When you've gone over the presentation a couple of times it feels more natural and you don't need to rely on a script. This allows you to respond more freely to the audience. That is why you're there."

Rutger was pleased with the presentation to his colleagues because it was well received by them. He thought it was going well while he was speaking because people got involved. He sensed their energy and their reactions. After the speech many colleagues gave him positive feedback. He's certain the success was down to the short, focused style of presentation.

It looks like those hockey lessons paid off.

Rutger's tips

- When using slides don't produce too many or too much text
- Be sparing in the use of figures/numbers
- Bring in some humour
- Be intuitive – do what you feel comfortable with – don't get pushed into using lecterns or other items

Linda James

Linda James is a familiar figure in the British film and television industry. She co-founded Red Rooster Film and Television Entertainment with Stephen Bayly in 1982. She headed up the company until 1998 when it was sold to Chrysalis Plc. She went on to co-found and float Alibi Communications Plc with Roger Holmes leading the company's production division until March 2003.

She is a prolific independent producer of over 20 award-winning drama series, five TV movies and two feature films. Linda has been Honorary Chair of the Edinburgh International Television Festival, a Governor of the British Film Institute (BFI), a Governor and Trustee of the National Film and Television School (NFTS), a member of the British Screen Advisory Council (BSAC), and she sat on the Independent Production Training Fund (IPTF) for the Producer's Alliance for Cinema and Television (PACT). She is currently the Chairperson of BAFTA'S Kids Committee and a member of BAFTA Council, Deputy Chair of the Children's Film and Television Foundation (CFTF) and sits on the board of Screen South for The Film Council. She is also a non-executive director of Alibi Communications Plc.

In 2004 she set up Sly Fox Films, a film and television production company, which re-unites her with Stephen Bayly, producer of the Oscar-nominated *Richard III* and *Mrs Dalloway* and Head of the National Film and Television School from 1998-2003. The company has a slate of feature film and television projects.

Linda's interview

It's not every day you do a pitch that makes the panel literally jump to their feet. But that's exactly what happened to leading independent television producer Linda James.

She was talking to two senior executives at Carlton Television ahead of the channel's launch. During the pitch her idea was given an instant green light for development. The show was a drama about the life of a young nun starring actress Kristin Scott Thomas. But why was the presentation so well received?

There were many reasons, most to do with the judgement and experience of Linda. Experience has taught her to go into meetings with a clear goal for your company and to make sure you ask for what you want.

An example of this occurred three weeks before that successful pitch. She attended a preliminary meeting where she carefully introduced something completely unexpected into the discussion. Already well known for her children's programmes she explained there was more she could do for the channel. She wanted to create opportunities for her company to make top notch primetime drama – and she did.

She came out of the pre-meeting with an opportunity to pitch for primetime drama. She had only three weeks to put the pitch together and didn't waste a second.

The preparation was intense. First there was the search for the right story. "We were looking for a strong narrative drama that had an image. It was a new channel and they did not want a police series, but something distinctive."

The story about the nun struck a chord immediately because it had all the hallmarks of great television. It had emotional development and a great saga. Linda felt the programme would refresh the schedule.

Its distinctiveness was also something the executives could use to market the programme to the public more easily. This is an increasingly important feature for today's television shows.

In the pitch Linda presented a single sheet of paper summarising her ideas for the benefit of the two executives. What Linda wanted to say was clearly formed in her mind and was reinforced with the benefit of mock pitch meetings. Nothing was left to chance.

The meeting started out routinely with a review of the channel's progress by the two television executives. Then it was over to Linda. As she started going through her ideas for the six-part drama Body and Soul energy levels soared in the meeting. "It was really good to see two grown men as excited as that – the idea was absolutely on target."

The drama was eventually made into a successful television series.

Typically during a meeting Linda will often ask "do you want me to tell you the story or would you prefer me to run through the slate? Most people say the story." Telling the story, Linda finds, is a powerful way of explaining a creative idea because it's so engaging for the listener.

And there are other ways that Linda uses the art of storytelling in a business presentation. She constructs her presentation with storytelling devices. The presentation will have a plot, moments of emotional engagement and counterpoints with humour.

If she detects lethargy in the meeting she will use the dramatic pause to regain attention. In business terms this often means a pause followed by a phrase such as "the important point is…". If that doesn't work she'll look at ways to change the atmosphere by introducing highs and lows or focusing on a human element of the proposed project.

The other technique that Linda uses when pitching is close observation.

Most of her pitches are one-to-one meetings. She says it's such an interpersonal moment that she's always looking at and responding to the smallest reactions. Things like the flicker of an eye can signal reservations or concerns.

"By drawing out reservations it means you're not working against the unseen. I enjoy the cut and thrust of the engagement and want to be sure I'm conveying my idea to the best of my ability."

But there are times when even your best efforts cannot rescue a difficult meeting. Linda recalls a pitch she did with a colleague to the BBC. The opening words of the television executive were something like, "we've got more good ideas than we can possibly produce and not enough openings for the shows that we want to make already – so tell me what your ideas are!"

It continued in a grim vein for a further 45 minutes. Because Linda was with a colleague felt she couldn't respond with a robust challenge. Instead she got through the meeting with as much dignity as she could.

What did she learn from that meeting? Today she would have interrogated the executive about what he meant by his opening remark. She would have been extremely careful not to be aggressive. She would have worked even harder to find some common ground with him to narrow down the issue to whatever it was. "It isn't worth conducting the meeting otherwise" she says.

Fortunately Linda learned lessons and quickly moved on. It wasn't long before she had television executives jumping to their feet!

Linda's tips

■ Make friends with your nerves. Nerves can help with adrenalin but they can also undermine what you're saying

■ Know what you want before a meeting

■ Find ways to engage your audience

■ Read your audience and respond

■ Don't apologise unnecessarily

■ Don't be unquestioning

Tony Buzan

Tony Buzan's interest in the functioning of the human brain had modest beginnings.

Buzan left England in the early 1960s for a course at the University of British Columbia. When he graduated with double honours in arts and science he expected a prestige job in business or academia.

Instead, an employment office offered him work in teaching or selling. He chose neither but then took a menial job in farming. More precisely, the work was digging out chicken manure, loading it on to a lorry and dumping it in the middle of a wood.

Yet Buzan found it was a great opportunity. He became physically fit, shovelling manure from 8am to 5pm, and was able to think. In the solitude of the farm he realised how fascinated he had become with the process of thinking itself.

A variety of other jobs followed, in banking, building, insurance and journalism. For three years he edited the international journal of Mensa. But his great love eventually became his career, and in 1987 he set up the Buzan Centres, promoting what he calls mental literacy. The term mind-mapping is now synonymous with Buzan's work.

His book *Use Your Head* is probably his best-known publication, one of more than 80 that he has written or co-written.

He is the co-founder of the Mind Sports Olympiad and founder of the World Memory Championships.

Today he travels widely and broadcasts regularly to put his brain message across. He claims to have been seen and heard by at least three billion people.

Tony's interview

Study the human brain. It's the first principle of getting the message across, says Tony Buzan. That cerebral view is probably what you'd expect from the man who's made a profession out of the efficient use of the brain and runs courses on the subject..

People tend to neglect the brain of the other party when they are trying to communicate, he says. "They think about technique, about themselves and about their message," he observes. "What they don't think about is brain-to-brain communication.

"You have to understand the brain of the person to whom you are speaking and their needs and goals, because if you don't you will be talking to a vacuum."

Most speakers throw their energies into producing a reasoned message, but often the words, though they make sense, are bland and unappealing.

For Buzan, however, an important pillar of the brain is the imagination, a function that uses all the human senses and should be on both the giving and receiving end of communications. It is fed by pictures and sensations. "We think in multi-sensual images," says Buzan. "Words are a sub-routine, they are the cargo-carriers for the images. And the person you are talking to is an infinitely capable image-making individual."

The presenter, of course, must understand the other person's brain well enough to know what images are needed to carry the message.

The conveying of images is not as difficult as one might think. If the message involves geography, for example, and Egypt is one of the subjects of the message, a mention of the Pyramids would establish the setting in the listener's mind. Talk about Paris and put forward the image of the Eiffel Tower. The setting of London can be imprinted on the mind by talk of St Paul's Cathedral.

Buzan then gets down to some more brass tacks and gives three further principles for an effective presentation.

Give some thought to the way you start the message. It is often said you never get a second chance to make a first impression. Buzan speaks of what he calls the Primacy Effect. The brain, he says, remembers more of what is said and done at the beginning of the listening period and pays more attention to it. This is the time to make that first impression. A dull start with no images for the brain to fix on blunts the impact of the presentation.

The second principle is the Recency Effect. This means the brain remembers the last things in a listening or learning period. As some would put it, you should go out on a high note.

The third principle is one of repetition, gently pushing the ideas home. The brain, says Buzan, needs about five well spaced repetitions throughout your presentation to commit them to long-term memory.

None of this comes without careful preparation. Be ready with images and metaphors and know when to repeat the salient points of the message that you want to stick.

There are other aids to the process of one brain getting across to another, and Buzan encourages the use of them. Again, the presenter must choose them carefully to be sure they are images that match and highlight the message. They can be illustrations flashed on to a screen or videos. They can also be movements. The speaker's turns and steps and gesticulations are important in backing up the message.

So Buzan makes it clear that the brain of one person can communicate with the brain of another by stimulating the multi-sensorial imagination.

"It's important to stay away from being only technical, logical, verbal, statistical and monochromatic," he says. The last is particularly important. Black and white images are too dull. Monochrome equals monotone, says Buzan. And monotone and its adjective monotonous mean boring.

Buzan then puts a human dimension on the process of brain-to-brain communication. "What you are doing is caring for the person to whom you are speaking," he says. He emphasises: "You are hosting the listener's mind."

To put it another way, you are mentally dancing with your listening partner, he says.

The Buzan way of conveying the message involves

- Understanding the brain of the person with whom you are communicating
- Creating images to highlight the message for the recipient
- Starting impressively
- Ending on a memorable note
- Repeating the important points several times during the presentation
- Using aids and body movement

Part two Media presentations

Jacqui's tips
- Get training
- Plan and rehearse your messages
- Focus on how you look

Talking to the media can make otherwise sensible people quite uncomfortable. It's something I encountered a lot when presenting TV news. I suppose it's partly to do with the busy nature of a newsroom. Everyone's on deadlines and split seconds count. There's pressure with a capital 'P'.

My best tip is to encourage you to get training from a company like my own before you talk to the media for the first time. It's not good for your business for you to learn how to do broadcast interviews on air.

There are other things you should always do. A good starting point is to know as much as possible about the programme. Find out the answers to the following questions:

- What's the story?
- What's my role?
- Is it a live interview or pre-record?
- How long will I be speaking?
- What's the style of the programme?
- What's the presenter/reporter like?

As well as covering the above you should be clear about the messages you want to get across. If there are much more than three you're probably not focused enough on your core messages. There will seldom be time to cover more than a few points. Make sure you say the ones that matter.

It's quite a skill to communicate well in the short time slots you get in news programmes. Rehearsing with a tape recorder or better still with a friend or colleague is always worthwhile.

Remember the camera can be merciless. Look your best. That means paying close attention to your hair and clothes. Make up is a must – even for men who generally just use powder to take off the shine on their face.

Michael Cole

Michael Cole got his training for dealing with the media by working inside the industry for many years.

His early days in print journalism gave way eventually to broadcasting. As a television journalist he was best known as the BBC's royal correspondent but he also covered six general elections, worked in 65 countries and reported from Beirut, Washington, the United Nations and southern Africa.

Later he gained his highest profile at Harrods, where he was the public affairs director from 1988 to 1998, and had a seat on the main board and on the boards of six subsidiary companies. It was the Harrods job that established him in the public mind, and he became adept at announcing even unpalatable facts with confidence and dignity.

After leaving Harrods Cole had his own talk show on the cable channel Living.

Today he runs his own media consultancy and is a non-executive director of six companies, including Lehmann Communications, an international public relations group. In addition, he has two associate directorships and is a consultant to a television production company, a financial consultancy and the British Heart Foundation.

Michael's interview

Ask Michael Cole how to deal with the media and he goes back a few paces first.

In a nutshell, the man who was the public face of Harrods for ten years says any organisation has to get its house in order before facing reporters and cameras. "Run your company in such a way that you are proud of its performance," he says.

For example, every company has environmental problems. Cole's advice: "Deal with them before they deal with you." What this means is that if you have settled your environmental problems they cannot be the subject of target practice for the media.

Cole often harks back to his experience at Harrods. Without waiting for a change in the law, the store decided to attach a 13-amp plug to every electrical appliance it sold so that novice purchasers could not fit the wiring wrongly and blow themselves up. Cole points out the moral of the tale with a good one-liner: "It's the sort of thing that says you care about the customer."

He then recalls one morning when Mohamed al-Fayed arrived in the store after a seeing a television programme about CFCs, the gases that knock an unhealthy hole in the ozone layer. The Harrods owner ordered all the machines and perfumes that used CFCs to be dispatched back to the suppliers – and promptly the rest of the industry followed suit.

Still on the environmental theme, Harrods rewired the 11,000 lights on the exterior of the Knightsbridge building with fibre optics, which use about a fifteenth of the electricity that conventional cables consume.

Clearly, Harrods with its house in order was making the image man's job simpler. Another one-liner puts it another way and relates the business dealings to the image: "Public relations will not do anything for an inferior product."

So, if the product is as good as it can be, how does Cole approach the media? "Journalists are not your friends or your enemies," he says. "They want one thing, which is a good story. If you give them a good story they're very happy."

He imagines a bunch of journalists being sent for a day to Lundy Island, which is practically deserted except for its lovable puffins. "The journalists would all come back that night with a story," he says.

Cole claims that, contrary to popular belief, journalists are not even interested in a free lunch. The story is all-important. With a good story the journalist can impress the editor, the editor can impress the proprietor, and the proprietor can impress the proprietor next door.

Cole's view of the media may sound brutal, even cynical. But his list of dos and don'ts makes it clear that his attitude to journalists face to face is one of respect and honesty. He advises anybody dealing with the media to treat journalists properly and never to patronise them. "Don't treat them as not being clever," advises Cole. "Instead, think of them as being as clever as you."

Although the public relations officer occupies the high ground in any confrontation or battle as he knows more about the subject than the journalist, the cardinal rule must be candour. "Always be as candid as possible," insists Cole. "Don't attempt to release only part of the information. Journalists will get the truth in the end." In the short term, he says, if you leave a vacuum the press will fill it with speculation.

If, however, you cannot tell the whole story, explain why.

He recalls the parallel cases of the capsizing of the *Herald of Free Enterprise* ferry off the Belgian coast at Zeebrugge in 1987, and the British Midland air crash on the M1 at Kegworth, Leicestershire, in 1989. The ferry disaster killed 193 people and 47 died in the air crash.

The chairman of P&O European Ferries and the head of British Midland had widely different reactions. While Peter Ford, the P&O man, is remembered for appearing remote in front of the television cameras, despite being conspicuous in his wide-brimmed hat, Sir Michael Bishop, the airline chairman, was seen taking charge and expressing regret straightaway. Bishop went on to head Channel 4. Such an appointment could have been recognition of the way he showed his face and managed the crisis.

The lesson: "People understand that mistakes happen. But they are not understanding when there is not sufficient contrition and apology where appropriate, and an immediate willingness to put things right."

If the problem in such circumstances is mishandled, as it was by P&O, public trust is undermined, and this, says Cole, is a prize that is hard to win and easy to lose.

Cole gives another example of openness with the press. Dingles, a Plymouth store that was part of the group to which Harrods belonged, was destroyed by fire. During the year in which Dingles was out of commission, Cole invited the press in constantly to observe the recovery process. He even allowed journalists to attend board meetings. That move must have been a world first. The openness had the double benefit of reinforcing the company's transparency and keeping the store's name in front of the public when normal business was impossible.

It also sets the tone for his attitude to commerce and its public image. "If I had a business," he says, "I would insist on two directors being on the site all the time – and being available."

For those who deal with the media Cole has a checklist

- Be available and prepare for interviews
- Take control
- Keep everything simple and avoid jargon
- Be candid
- Listen before speaking
- Apologise if at fault
- Honour your commitments – Cole recalls he had a long list of press men and women to telephone after Princess Diana and Dodi al-Fayed were killed in that Paris car crash, but he called every one of them back

Cary Cooper CBE

Britain has become home for the American psychologist Cary Cooper since he arrived in 1964.

He was actually born in Hollywood in 1940 and named after Cary Grant. That is where the connection with the actor ends.

Cooper attended a university in California and crossed the Atlantic to finish his studies at Leeds University.

He became a social psychology lecturer at Southampton University but in 1972 his association with Manchester started. He was head-hunted by the late Professor Sir Roland Smith, then head of Manchester Business School, to move north.

He became Bupa professor of organisational psychology and health at the University of Manchester Institute of Science and Technology and was in that post until 2003, when he was appointed to a similar position at Lancaster University Management School.

His efforts in the field of organisational psychology have now been recognised. In the 2001 Queen's Birthday Honours he was made a CBE for his contribution.

Cooper has written or co-written more than 100 books on business psychology, occupational stress and the role of women in work and holds honorary doctorates at four British universities.

With a fellow professor he set up Robertson Cooper, a business psychology company, whose projects have included a stress audit for the Treasury. The two professors started the business in 2000, and by 2004 it was expected to show a profit.

Cary's interview

Academics as a breed just shy away from the media. So meet the exception to the rule, Cary Cooper, media-friendly and always prepared to give an honest view on things.

Cooper has been the Bupa professor of organisational psychology and health at the University of Manchester Institute of Science and Technology. The serious-sounding title belies the outgoing personality of a man who puts across business behaviour ideas in an easy manner without a hint of jargon.

His readiness is, sadly, not typical of the reaction that journalists bump up against when they call Britain's colleges and universities.

"A lot of the media do come to academics," says Cooper, "and academics are frightened of them."

The problem according to Cooper is that those frequently approached and normally mild-mannered academics are not trained to respond to press and television journalists and they fear they will be misrepresented.

Part of the trouble is the even-handedness that is the order of the day. It is second nature for academics to look at issues from all sides and be neutral, possibly because they are teachers. "They want to sit on the fence," says Cooper.

Yet as intelligent people they must have an opinion. "They are just too frightened to make a judgment call," says Cooper.

Cooper's advice to the reticent is to come out of their shell. The head-on approach is much more acceptable to the media. "I try to tell them what I actually think," says Cooper. "I try not to pull punches."

The policy of directness is equally recommended to an academic who does not give an answer because he cannot base it on the careful research that is the profession's stock in trade. Cooper's attitude: "If I don't know, I say I don't know."

Even then, he says, he would venture an off-the-cuff opinion. He would make it clear that he did not have all the facts to work on but that he tended to have a certain view drawn from the information to hand.

Cooper realises there is a downside to his openness with the media. "From time to time the media will distort what you say," he concedes, "and it is usually because they make mistakes, not because they want to misrepresent you deliberately."

So he accepts the occasional distortion and regards it as a small price to pay for his willingness to communicate.

He regrets that there is little research on how to deliver information effectively. Authoritative studies would help the fearful and the reluctant communicators. For this reason Cooper's university introduced a corporate communications degree course in 2001.

As it happens, his advice on speaking to the media can be applied to the corporate field. This is his area of expertise after all.

He believes large companies could avoid much of the mud-slinging about fat cat remuneration that has marked the start of the 21st century. He observes a "big communications gap" at the top of British companies that leads to embarrassment and anger among shareholders and in the wider public arena.

The directors of large companies often announce or admit that they are to lavish £20 million packages on chief executives without saying why. And that is their big mistake.

Cooper tells them to explain their reasoning behind huge cash deals. The explanation will not wash with everybody but it could soften the blow and cut down the bitter, damaging publicity that follows shareholders' meetings.

Some huge bounties are dolled out to keep highly competent officers in the company. The bosses are often scared that without piles of money their key man or woman will defect to the United States, where they will get enormous bucks. This was exactly the argument advanced by the huge HSBC banking organisation for offering a multi-million-pound package to one of its directors. Even this generous deal would barely put him in the top 50 in the American executive pay league, explained Keith Whitson, the HSBC chief executive. Whitson did the right thing in setting out the detail behind the bank's decision.

"One reason why the transparent policy is often missing is that the corporate communications experts advising the company are less than expert," says Cooper. First, companies have to choose their advisers well.

Then they need to heed the advice. "Corporate communications experts are just not listened to enough," he says.

The result, he observes, is that many company bosses cover up the unpalatable news. But he points out: "I think people respect the truth. It is much better when they are given an explanation."

Many times directors blame the company's ills on a general economic depression. This cuts little ice with Cooper, who believes the people at the top have a responsibility to foresee trends and troubles and take action. Only then can they offload the blame.

The same principles apply inside the workplace, he says, but generally communication here is appalling. The great gap starts at board level, so that messages and information do not move even from the top floor to the senior management, says Cooper.

The directors do themselves no favours by being so remote. They have a responsibility to hold the same system of values as those who work with them, believes Cooper. "These senior people don't walk and talk enough. They distance themselves from their own corporate culture," he says.

A bright light in all this darkness, he says, is Greg Dyke, the former BBC Director General, who made a point of going to the coalface and visiting BBC units all over the country.

A final warning from the business psychology professor: "If you don't tell the truth people will go searching for it."

Any tips for the company man or woman who needs to present information? Cooper has three simple ones

- Communicate clearly
- Always tell the truth
- Don't be covert and secretive

David Brewerton

The business world has played a vital part in David Brewerton's working life.

For 17 years he was a business and investment writer with *The Daily Telegraph*. When *The Independent* newspaper was launched he became its first city editor.

His third experience of the broadsheet press was with *The Times*, where he was the business editor for three years.

He switched in 1991 from writing the news to releasing it, becoming a partner in the London public relations company Brunswick. Here he developed his skills in handling the bad news along with the good.

Brewerton retired in 2003 and is happily engaged in what all journalists promise themselves they will do. He is writing a book. He says it will be a novel illustrating and explaining why the media behaves as it does and why it prefers conspiracy theories to simple facts.

David's interview

The public relations executive brought into a crisis at a client company must feel like mouthing the cliché: "It's a dirty job but somebody's got to do it."

David Brewerton probably had that feeling a few times during his years with the large London public relations organisation Brunswick. "I often had the tricky ones," he says from the haven of retirement.

He recalls the client whose employee in the United States took enough out of the till to affect the company results, and the publisher whose magazine circulation had been overstated so that advertisers were overcharged. He thinks of the pharmaceuticals company whose product was found to contain impurities, and the employers who had to sack workers by the crowd.

The problems often came without warning and the public relations man had to move fast to minimise the damage to the company and the impact on the share price. Soon the media and the shareholders would be demanding to know things, and the presentation of the facts would be so important. Brewerton would go back to basic principles.

Much of his work was in the preparation. "Anyone with bad news has to take it very seriously indeed," he says. The advice is not as obvious as it seems. Think of the directors who shut the door on reporters or avoid blunt questions, hoping nobody will notice. "Some directors don't like to face up to what they have to do," says Brewerton.

The company should hurry to bring in its relevant key advisers. They could be lawyers, brokers, merchant bankers. If money is missing, the auditors have to be called. The experts should certainly include the public relations consultants.

The next move: "Gather every last scrap of information internally," says Brewerton. "The worst thing is when the outside world knows something of which you are not aware. It makes you look either shifty or incompetent. You must make sure you have better information than the people who come knocking on your door asking difficult questions."

Who's going to face the media? A senior executive director was Brewerton's choice. "I have always thought the chief executive or chairman is not there just for the good news," he says.

Some of the questions can be anticipated. How did this crisis happen and what are you going to do about it? It's worth rehearsing the answers as far as possible.

Somebody will ask whether heads will roll. At that stage the stock and honest reply has to be that it is too early to say.

These events are usually one-offs. The man at the front must emphasise this. Catastrophes are not common occurrences, so he has to make clear that if money has been lifted from the till it is not going to bankrupt the company. The organisation is still trading and it is still the same organisation. The crisis must be kept in proportion.

Through all this the company must show that it is competent and is taking action. Whatever happens – and the sticky questions are bound to be asked – the company's spokesperson must stay calm.

When a company hits a crisis the directors may think that the best impression will be created if they give an exclusive to a publication known to be friendly to their company.

Bad idea, says Brewerton. When the friendly publication has put the story in a favourable light the other publications will descend with fury. Their noses will have been put out of joint because they have missed the story and they will want to dig for dirt. The favourable publicity will turn sour.

Another temptation is to "bury bad news". The company may think 6pm is a good time because the national daily press will be too busy to bother with it. Or perhaps it would be good to break the story just as the government is announcing shattering figures on cancer or telling the nation that half a dozen new motorways are to be built.

It's a ploy that is destined not to work. The bad news will be snapped up, a little late perhaps, but it will be compounded by allegations that somebody tried to slide it through unnoticed.

It is best to make the announcement at 9am in an orderly fashion, without trickery and without giving exclusives. The music has to be faced and the transparent method limits the number of wounds the company will suffer.

When the story has been well and truly aired, that friendly publication can be approached, advises Brewerton. An honest briefing with a serious-minded, even-handed newspaper can repair some of the damage and restore confidence.

Brewerton has a few more tips for dealing with the tricky jobs during the crisis and in the aftermath.

"Never get rattled," he says. "Don't ever get into a telephone-slamming situation with a journalist." Irate directors are known to play the hard man in this way but the violent reaction weakens their case. Brewerton advises that the company should keep talking with the media. "In that way you still have some influence over what is going to be published," he says.

When the heat is on directors are tempted to reach for their lawyers. They hope to gag the newspapers by asking the High Court for an injunction. It is rarely sensible, says Brewerton. "You are unlikely to get the injunction," he says, "but if you do, you then advertise the story because newspapers have to be told about it."

Then comes the worst bit. When the injunction goes and the wraps come off the story, the newspapers will pounce with greed, making the damage far worse.

Job losses are a special case when the company comes to present its news. Brewerton says: "Timing is crucial. A lot of people have to be told, including the market and the media. The order in which you do that is important."

First, the heads of the workforce should be told overnight. The human resources people have to know at the same time.

The workforce must be informed when they arrive for the morning shift and the others should have letters on their doormats. "The last thing you want is to have employees hearing the news on television or radio before they have been told," says Brewerton.

Then tell the media, and be ready with all the facts – details of retraining packages and redundancy terms, for example.

A final word from the man who has had his fair share of tough assignments? "A lot of it is common sense, and not being afraid of the problem and grasping it."

How to do it, the Brewerton way

- Do your homework and have your information at your fingertips
- Put a well rehearsed senior executive in front of the media
- Stay calm, keep the crisis in proportion
- Be transparent and don't try to slip the news out furtively
- Tell the people who are affected first – timing is crucial

Part three After dinner speaking

Jacqui's tips
- Know the agenda inside out if you're hosting
- Match the mood of the audience
- Keep business messages light

I have hosted many after dinner events. I often host the whole evening or a section, for example an awards slot. They can be good fun but like any other presenting role they require preparation.

I relax a lot more if I have a running order. It's a TV term that refers to a detailed agenda. Strangely if things don't go according to plan and we have to adapt things I find it easier if I've got a running order to scribble on. I like to rehearse so that the polish is there. And I insist on very detailed briefing so I can do a good job.

There is a very different feel to these type of events. It's quite convivial and so it's important to match the mood of the occasion. A relaxed and friendly presenting style usually works for me. I keep things brief and bring lots of light touches to the event.

I always consider how I should dress for an event. In the evening it's often appropriate to go quite glam – I love it!

I'm not an entertainer but I usually get to introduce the entertainment or the speaker and I talk them up as much as I dare.

Bob Bevan MBE

Bob 'the Cat' Bevan is one of the top after-dinner speakers in the country. He has won numerous awards for his speeches including: The Reuters Jackie Blanchflower Memorial Trophy, The Benedictine After Dinner Speakers Award and the *Mail on Sunday* After Dinner Speakers Hall of Fame.

He has worked with many comedians including Jasper Carrott, Jimmy Tarbuck and Bruce Forsyth. In the music world he has worked with many stars including The Bee Gees, Elton John and Rod Stewart.

Bob previously had careers in journalism and public relations. He was a reporter on *Lloyd's List*, the daily shipping newspaper, and deputy editor of a travel trade magazine. He was also group director of public relations for European Ferries for 14 years and has run his own PR consultancy. He made his first speech at his old boys dinner in 1967 and turned professional in 1980.

Sport is Bob's great love. He played football for West Wickham in the Southern Amateur League and Old Wilsonians in the Southern Olympian League for 25 years and still plays in veteran games. Before going in goal he was an inside forward. He is a Trustee of the major cricket-based charity The Lord's Taverners, and Honorary Barker in the Variety Club and a Member of the Grand Order of Water Rats.

Bob is the author of *Nearly Famous – Adventures of an After Dinner Speaker*.

Bob's interview

Sheer poetry. That's how one of the country's leading after dinner speakers wowed his audience. In 1999 Bob 'the Cat' Bevan used his humorous poetry for the roasting of the Duke of Edinburgh. The gag is based on the idea that despite meeting the Duke of Edinburgh about 12 times "those meetings have been far more memorable for me than they appear to have been for him." Below is an extract from that poem.

The Duke and I

I'd like to test our 12th man's memory
We first met back in 1983
He knew Frankie Howerd and Frank Carson
He'd even heard of Nicholas Parsons
But he didn't recognise me

The Variety Club is another good cause
I spoke in his honour and drew some applause
And as he started to go
He did say "cheerio"
But I don't think he knew who I was

I went to Windsor, which is a bit of a hike
Too far to go on me bike
I commentated after tea
Then as he walked by me
I heard him say "who's that bloke on the mike?"

© Bob Bevan 2004 from his book *Nearly Famous*, published by Virgin Books, September 2003.

This ditty continues for several more verses. The impact of the poem is strengthened by Bob's delivery. His great timing and straight-faced demeanour got resounding royal approval and brought the house down at the 50th anniversary of the Lord Taverner's charity.

And there are many other examples of his success. Bob has won countless awards for his after dinner presentations including the *Mail on Sunday's* After Dinner Speakers Hall of Fame. He is also well known for his television appearances on the BBC's Auntie's Sporting Bloomers. But you might not know that singer Rod Stewart also raves about Bob's speaking skills after booking Bob for his dad's 80th birthday party.

So how did the Cat (as he's usually known) excel in this field? Simple, he followed advice from Hollywood actor Michael Caine at a masterclass. Michael said "steal from everyone." Michael was encouraging performers to watch other people's mannerisms especially those you admire. The mannerisms you adopt don't come out the same as anybody else's so no-one really knows you've stolen them.

The people Bob admired are some of Britain's top comedians. He describes Eric Morecambe, Jasper Carrot and Tommy Cooper as his heroes. He observed how Jasper used to shake his head in disbelief at what he'd just said. Tommy Cooper laughed only when the audience was laughing. His timing was fantastic.

But the turning point came when Bob followed some crucial advice. He was told he would be much funnier if he kept a straight face. He promptly took this on board and found it worked well for him. He noticed big improvements when watching videos of his performances.

As a professional after dinner speaker Bob has plenty of advice for business people who find themselves frequently taking part in such events. The first thing to establish is whether you're any good at telling jokes. "If not, it's better not to try too hard. Focus on the five or six key points that you're trying to get over."

Personalising the presentation by referring to members of the audience also works well. Bob will often take the mickey out of members of the audience but has a few words of caution here. It's got to be appropriate, that is, not offend the people or the audience. It's also important for everyone in the audience to know the people being singled out. Otherwise not everyone in the room will be in on the gag "and that's bad news for any presenter."

When it comes to rehearsing your presentation Bob recommends three run-throughs and rehearsing everything. That includes how someone else introduces you, how you walk on and walk off and being familiar with the type of microphone you'll be using. "Things mustn't look messy or unprofessional to staff, right down to handing over mikes, otherwise the moment can inadvertently become a comic moment."

And what can you do when things are not going well? Bob's advice is to keep going until you get back on track. Bob always has a couple of really strong jokes on standby that he can turn to if it all starts to go a bit sour. But in such a situation it's important to be self aware. Be honest with yourself - is the situation beyond repair? If so, then it's time for the Harry Hill solution: "if you're going badly – get off. If you're going well – get off."

He also takes the view that all presenters come unstuck at some stage. The really good ones learn from their mistakes and carry on. Bob also says that with experience you become pretty philosophical. A 95% rate of success is fairly acceptable for anybody in any kind of working life.

As the scriptwriter for former Conservative Party leader William Hague, Bob has tips for anyone using scripts. It's important if somebody is writing your scripts to make sure they coach you through the content so you can deliver it really well. Give plenty of time to get to know the material and work collaboratively with the writer. Go out to lunch – take plenty of time to read it through and to feel the material.

He remembers the most successful script he did for William Hague. After reading the script he went to lunch with William Hague and a couple of colleagues. Obviously they had the material to look at but they spent the afternoon telling jokes and from that they kept refining their material. Bob found the material just got better and better.

One of Bob's favourite one liners for William Hague was done at the expense of Prime Minister Tony Blair in the House of Commons. It was a reference to Tony Blair being all jokes and no substance. Bob gave William Hague the one-liner "at least my jokes are quite good – all yours are in the cabinet."

Bob's tips

- Use other people's mannerisms and styles where appropriate
- Use audience members to personalise your speech
- Rehearse three times
- When using scripts work collaboratively with the writer to make the most of the material

Richard Blackwood

Richard completed a BA in Business Studies before turning his hand to comedy. He has since performed in comedy venues up and down the country. He is also a regular at the famous Comedy Store in London's West End.

He has fronted many television shows including The Richard Blackwood Show (1999/2001) for Channel 4, MTV's Select (1997/2001), Club Class, a stand-up comedy show for Channel 5 and the Paramount Comedy Channel (1997). He also presented The Base (1997) – one of MTV's top ten shows and two series of *Togs*, a Channel 5 programme (1997/8).

He has been a regular presenter on Top of the Pops. Richard was also the bar manager in *The Club* which was transmitted on the ITV network

Richard had two top ten hits *Mama, Who Da Man* and *1,2,3,4, Get with the Wicked*, featuring Chilean rapper Deetah and General Levy.

Richard's awards include the top television personality award from BICA (the Black International Comedy Awards), the best satellite programme award from TV Hits Awards 2000 for Select and he was nominated for a Brits Award in 2001. Richard has also received a Peoples Choice Award from the Black Music Awards and the top UK Personality from the Cable TV Awards.

Richard made his acting debut in the BBC comedy/drama Ed Stone Is Dead in which he starred. He has also signed a holding deal with Fox Network in Los Angeles.

Richard is a patron of Body & Soul, an organisation that supports children and teenagers living with or affected by HIV/Aids.

Richard's interview

There's no doubt in the mind of top comedian Richard Blackwood that it's the start of a presentation that counts.

Whether he's doing a stand up routine to a live audience or presenting to millions of people on television, he pays particular attention to the beginning. "As a comedian you always open with a very strong joke" says Richard "because you know the positive response you're going to get and you need that to get going."

Richard often adapts his openers to suit different events. He recalls a live Awards Show he hosted for the British Academy of Film and Television Arts (BAFTA) in 2002 where he went for something completely different. He started the show with a rap song! Richard was pleased with this event because it was a real challenge for him.

He admits he wasn't totally comfortable with the idea of doing the rap song. Although he can sing, and has released records with rap artists, he sees himself as a comedian. He worked on the song for three days beforehand.

But the hard work paid off. He received lots of good feedback from the audience and was particularly pleased with congratulations from television producer and presenter Floella Benjamin OBE.

The preparation Richard did for this presentation to over 800 people involved more than working on the rap song. Richard paid close attention to the scripts. In fact he rewrote all the scripts so they sounded much more like his natural speaking style. Richard believes getting the autocue script up to scratch is crucial because at a live event you have only one opportunity to get it right.

However, Richard limits his reliance on autocue and really dislikes when things are totally scripted, including ad libs. He prefers to 'freestyle' which means he departs from the script when he feels it's appropriate. You have to be pretty confident as a presenter to do that because it's very easy to lose your way in the script.

Richard rehearsed other sequences in the show including a chat sequence with the television fox puppet, Basil Brush (this was the BAFTA Children's Awards!). He wanted to feel really comfortable with that element of the show because he was uncertain how the audience would receive it. Luckily people were laughing at the jokes and paying close attention.

What other tips does he have for business presenters – particularly those doing after dinner presentations?

He believes you must take care of your attitude. You must go into the presentation "believing in what you're capable of." You should also work on your delivery skills and think carefully about how you convey the information. The success of the presentation is not determined by the information given as much as how that information is put across.

Richard has a word of warning about delivery technique. "Don't overcompensate. Work within the realms you have. Be careful not to go overboard." He believes if you're honest with yourself about your weaknesses in delivery you can usually reduce the impact of your shortcomings. For example, if you don't speak loudly – make sure you go close to the microphone and work on projection.

Richard says business professionals have much to gain by being honest with their audience if things get tricky. They're already successful in their field. They can be straight with their audience about how they're feeling, for example saying, "I am extremely nervous – but let's give it a go." Adopting this strategy is more likely to get presenters through a minor difficulty and allow them to get on with the rest of the presentation.

Making business information interesting to an audience is a constant challenge. One way to do this is to make the audience laugh. But how do you make something funny? Richard's advice is to focus on something that strikes you as funny. Then trust in the way it's funny to you and try to convey that to your audience.

Your main weapon here is timing. That's the key to making people laugh. Spend as much time as you can getting your timing right. Richard cites television presenter Jonathan Ross as a great example. "He's not a stand-up comedian but he's got perfect timing. He knows exactly where to laugh. Remember, you can introduce humour to almost anything with good timing."

When a show is not going to plan Richard has a few tips. If things are only mildly astray Richard will use the power of his voice. Sometimes simply raising his voice is enough to rescue the situation. However, if things are really tough he will tell the audience the show's nearly over. In other situations he's singled out someone in the audience and gently poked fun at them. The diversion can work a treat. "You've got to trust that the audience doesn't know what's happening next. The important thing is feeling you're back in control."

Pacing a presentation will also help when things take an unexpected turn for the worse. Richard describes controlling your pace as like being in a boxing bout. No champion fighter boxes hard all the way. Instead the champ saves his energy to deliver the knockout blow when the opponent is waning. Similarly a presenter should save the 'fireworks' for when the audience is less attentive.

For a business presenter that means paying close attention to the content of your presentation. Make a critical assessment to gauge how the audience is likely to react to different elements of the presentation.

To achieve excellence in presentation skills Richard feels you have to be prepared for some things not working perfectly in your presentation. If you're flexible and in tune with your audience you can usually find another way to stay with them. Trial and error can be a great tutor.

And how important are the right clothes for an after dinner presentation? To Richard it's part of the preparation. Richard goes to present a show looking "'well dressed, presentable, and stylish." He'll often choose a smart suit with a modern cut − but he's not into designer labels. And he's not dressed by an army of stylists because he knows how he wants to look and what looks good on him.

So once you've got the beginning of your presentation sorted, it's time to pay attention to the end. Richard always saves his best joke for the closer.

Richard's tips

- Make a strong start
- Rewrite scripts to your own speaking style
- Work on your timing
- Be flexible if things aren't working out

Marilyn Orcharton

A newspaper once called Marilyn Orcharton Scotland's First Lady of Business. Modestly, she says she can't remember which newspaper it was.

Although management consultancy is now her specialisation, she spent 20 years of her working life as a dentist. It was this experience that led her into the ground-breaking business Denplan in 1986. Marilyn was one of the founders of the scheme under which patients pay an annual fee and receive most types of dental treatment without further charge.

Denplan became highly successful but Marilyn sold her interest in 1992 to start a new business, Kite Consultants, in Glasgow.

This business is now called Isoplan. It provides management software, mainly for dentists and nursing homes at present, but Marilyn expects to introduce it soon to other professionals, including pharmacists, veterinary surgeons and hairdressers.

To earn her title she was the first woman President of the Glasgow Chamber of Commerce in 1999 and was for two years Chairman of the Small Business Bureau. She remains a director of that organisation.

Marilyn's interview

There is one fundamental thing you have to know if you want to deliver after-dinner speeches. Speaking is not a soft option, however easy it may look when you are on the receiving end and bloated with steak or Christmas pud.

After years in business Marilyn Orcharton has made a speciality of this fine art but says she is misunderstood even by her own family. "They think I do it from the back of an envelope," she says. "Yet it takes a while to get confidence."

The second basic lesson is that one size does not fit all. The same speech cannot be pulled off the shelf for every occasion. That's the lazy way and it also guarantees you'll die on your feet most times.

If the stock speech won't do for everybody, what's the drill? Do your homework so that you can hit the right note. That's Marilyn's third basic lesson for after-dinner presenting.

"The golf club captain who organises the occasion doesn't understand that you haven't got a set speech," says Marilyn. "But the speaker has to cross-examine these people. What age group are the guests? Are they men or women? How many of them are in business? You find all audiences are different."

Tailor your speech to the audience, get it right from the outset and there's a fair chance you won't suffer disaster and stomach-turning humiliation.

As a proud Scot Marilyn does her share of Burns supper speeches, but even these events attract groups as diverse as the colours of Joseph's coat.

She recalls a Burns supper for a junior section of the Royal Institution of Chartered Surveyors. The guests were all aged under 35, and although the supper was in honour of Scotland's greatest poet, they knew nothing about Burns. At the speechifying stage of the evening they probably didn't give a damn either.

"By the time I rose to speak they were all out of their box," says Marilyn. "They just wanted a few jokes." Obviously, it was not a case of meeting at 7.30 for 8. It was more one of gathering at 5 for 9. So after all the booze had been sloshed down, the young professionals were hardly in a mood for considering the subtleties of fine verse.

Those jokes, too, are vitally important. Never ask why the after-dinner speaker's sleeve is bulging. It's full of funny stories that have been pushed up it. "Always keep a string of jokes in reserve," advises Marilyn.

Her Burns night speech to a bunch of accountants was a different affair altogether: "I had to make it relevant to Burns."

When Marilyn spoke at a lunch held by the Nottingham Chamber of Commerce the Ryder Cup had just finished. The golf tournament was a natural topical subject, but for these traders a business slant was required. The slant would have been a more sporty one if she had been speaking to a golf club dinner.

The women's section of a golf club was different again and must have been quite a challenge to Marilyn the businesswoman. Most of these ladies of leisure had never been employed, so business-oriented anecdotes would have fallen as flat as Holland. Nevertheless, funny stories there had to be. Polite, comfortable ones.

Marilyn carefully avoided the mistake committed by the toastmaster at this dinner. The poor man barged in with risqué gags, to which the dear ladies reacted like a cemetery full of tombstones. Not a titter. Marilyn assumed he had not researched his audience, but maybe he hadn't even given it a thought.

An important tip for telling jokes – be careful if you are using other people's. Perhaps you decide to steal a story that Ken Dodd told because it made you split your sides and everything else at the same time. You, however, may tell it without the Doddy appeal and end up looking like a chump. It literally is the way the comedian tells 'em that makes them work.

Marilyn is always wary of a pie-eyed audience, like those well-oiled young surveyors. "If they're all drunk don't try to be clever," she says. Dinner guests lose patience if they have to think. They just want to be entertained and to guffaw.

There is, of course, plenty of scope with the more laid-back worldly-wise audience. For example, people love to have a laugh at their leader's expense.

Therefore, as part of her research Marilyn often tries to discover something about, say, the chairman. A little weakness maybe. She then tells a story that illustrates the foible, a tale that tickles the audience's ribs without offending the victim.

She finds that women and students are the most difficult audiences. Women whose lives have lacked the experience of the workplace need a particularly customised speech, but students are dangerous listeners because they take a cynical approach. They regard the speech as another college lecture and try to outsmart the speaker.

The earlier advice applies here, says Marilyn. Get them on your side right away and you have got them.

Marilyn often does it with a self-deprecating story. She says: "I tell them my name is Marilyn but people call me Jeanie. Somebody will ask whether that is because I'm Scottish. 'Oh, no,' I say, 'it's because I always appear when somebody opens a bottle'."

The Jeanie-genie quip usually wins them over.

One huge mistake that must be avoided like a contagion is outstaying your welcome by droning on. "Limit your speech to 20 or 30 minutes," says Marilyn. "Billy Connolly could go on for longer and get away with it, but most of us can't. Be prepared, too, to cut your speech if it is lasting too long or if the evening appears to be dragging."

An experience that proved the point for Marilyn was a speech given at a dentists' dinner by Edwina Currie when she was a health minister.

Mrs Currie should have expected a hard time as all dentists were in a rebellious mood at the time. The speech was punctuated by catcalls, and when her frustration boiled over into words she blurted out that the speech had not been written by her. A civil servant, she said, had written the displeasing words – and, embarrassingly, he happened to be there with her.

Relentlessly she plodded on and read the prepared speech until the final full stop. "She had not got the ability to change it," says Marilyn. "If the speech doesn't go down well you have got to switch it around."

Mrs Currie left in tears. Oh, dear. She might have avoided all that by following Marilyn's recipe of research, adapt, empathise, joke and change direction when necessary.

Marilyn's top tips for aspiring after-dinner speakers

- Know your audience
- Listen to what other speakers have said to blend in with the spirit of the occasion
- Keep an eye on the time so you don't bore or irritate your audience

Part four Motivational speaking

Jacqui's tips
- Find a speaking style that suits you
- Use anecdotes
- Find ways to keep your material fresh

Talking about my life as a black woman, a television presenter or a businesswoman is something I get called upon to do. Although quite a private person I feel very uplifted when the audience connect to my life story.

The presentation style I use for motivational speaking is very similar to how I presented my chat show on television. I keep it relaxed, upbeat and professional.

The feel is conversational so I usually have very few notes – maybe some key words written on a small index card. That gives me a structure without being too rigid. I do usually write something down to keep me on target.

People are always interested in my life in television. They want to know about the personalities I worked with and the job of presenting news programmes.

I often talk about my first day at the BBC. I was so nervous I ran into the loo and bumped into Esther Rantzen! Then there was my first news bulletin. I will never forget the moment the red light went on and I was live on air. The mixture of fear and intense excitement was electric. Somehow I managed to deliver the bulletin and that was the start of my television career.

The challenge with motivational speaking is keeping the material fresh even though you've said it many many times before. I do this by making sure I change the beginning and end of every presentation. I also change my anecdotes and examples to suit the audience I'm talking to.

Simon Weston

Simon Weston became one of Britain's most recognisable faces after suffering severe burns during the Falklands War in 1982. Many men were lost and wounded when the *Sir Galahad* was bombed, but it was Simon's story that grabbed everybody's attention.

It was fame that he had never expected. Simon was born in Nelson, Mid-Glamorgan in 1961. He joined the Welsh Guards in 1978 and served in Berlin, Northern Ireland and Kenya. Then came the Falklands and the serious burns that required plastic surgery and which changed his life.

Simon's story was told in a television documentary and he rose to the status of national celebrity. However, he has built on that fame by founding a charity called Weston Spirit. The aims of the charity, based in Liverpool, are best put in Simon's own words: "It encourages young people to believe in their potential and worth and value to society and to themselves."

The Royal British Legion and the Royal Star and Garter Home for disabled ex-servicemen are other causes in which Simon takes an interest. He has also written autobiographical books and works of fiction.

He lives in Cardiff, "the finest place in the cosmos", with his wife and children. In 1992 he was made an OBE for his charity work.

Simon's interview

As motivational speakers go, Simon Weston conveys a simple and obvious message. He puts himself forward as an example, without the psycho-babble, obscurity and jargon that some motivational spouters use to gush at an audience of people who have unwisely parted with their money to listen.

To be more precise, Simon says the examples he offers are of himself and the people who have supported him during and since his recovery from the appalling trauma he suffered on the *Sir Galahad*.

Simon's own example is impressive, of course. He says in his own resilient way: "Just because something bad has happened to you, do not just stop. Many people say, 'What an awful thing.' But just look at the reality of it. The experience brought great pain but it also brought me a great deal of success. It has allowed me to meet my wife, it has brought me my kids, and I have a comfortable lifestyle."

In effect, a motivational speech by Simon is a speech about himself. "It's the easiest thing in the world to speak about what you are," he says. So when he stands up to speak he tells people that they can achieve their goals in much the same way as he rose above a devastating experience to build a new life.

Yet there are a few rules to observe if a speaker is to motivate an audience to show the kind of determination that Simon Weston has.

He has a few choice words about the rules: "Be honest, be forthright and speak about what you know and what you believe in. There's no point in giving people bull. It is said you can fool some of the people some of the time, but you can't fool all of the people all of the time.

"Anyway, I'm a lousy liar. Just ask my wife!"

Simon starts his motivational addresses with a two-minute film that introduces him and his life to his audience. He takes into account that there may be some for whom the Falklands War is not even a personal memory. For others the memory may be a dim one.

Then he speaks for 30 or 45 minutes and shows another short film about himself. This is the real visual motivator. "It shows what you can do," says Simon.

He follows this with a few more minutes of talking to prompt a question and answer session. And this, he says, is a way of showing respect to the audience. He explains: "People have the right to choose when you are giving a speech. If they want me to stay there for an hour, that's what I do. The job is always according to whatever I can give people."

Being at the disposal of the audience is clearly key to Simon's presentations. He realises that an address raises questions to which the people in the hall want answers. "There are always more questions than answers," observes Simon, "and the more you know the more you realise you need to know."

It is therefore only right and caring to give listeners the time to obtain answers to their questions. It is part of the respect. "I feel I am serving the people to whom I am speaking," says Simon.

The serious and worthy approach, however, has to have a lighter touch. "You have just got to introduce humorous anecdotes," says Simon. A rule of thumb, though, is not to be too subtle with your gags. He finds that younger people don't generally get the subtle type of joke.

To Simon the whole presentation is uplifting, from the first film, through the speech to the questions and answers. A good motivational session sends people home still thinking. "I find this inspirational stuff rewarding," he says. "You are stimulating debate."

If people are to be travelling home with thoughts and arguments going through their heads, does Simon do it with a big finish? "Oh, no," he says. "I'm not that predictable. I have to change the speech and the ending every time. You see, I've got to enjoy doing it as well."

Simon cannot be precise about how to sign off but the point about enjoying giving the address is well made. Simon says: "People are far smarter than some may think. If you are bored doing the speaking, it is going to come through. If *you* are bored, the people are going to be *really* bored. And you don't want them to go away saying how boring he was."

He has to think when asked to describe his best experience as a speaker. Then he recalls: "I spoke once to 9,000 people in Birmingham. At the end of the speech they got up and gave me a standing ovation. Yes, that just about does it."

Did he feel he had finally succeeded when that happened? He becomes modest. "I never feel I have succeeded," he replies. "But I am succeeding."

Simon's tips for success

- Set an example yourself if you want to motivate others
- Be honest
- Be forthright
- Talk about what you know
- Stay as long as people want you – they have come to see you, after all
- Make 'em laugh
- Enjoy it yourself

Roger Black MBE

Roger Black represented Britain at the highest level in athletics for 14 years. His specialities were the 400 metres and the 4 x 400 metres relay race.

Athletics, in fact, determined the course of his life from an early age. Roger was born in Portsmouth in 1966 and educated at Portsmouth Grammar School. He gained a place to read medicine at Southampton University in 1985. By then, however, he had already shown where his talents lay and he decided to rescind his place to concentrate on his track and field career.

Six years later he was to receive an honorary degree from the university.

In his time he picked up 15 major championship medals, including European, Commonwealth and World Championship golds, and was the British men's team captain. He is best known for gaining a silver medal in the 400 metres at the 1996 Olympic Games, but this came after he had undergone five surgical operations.

After his athletics achievements Roger became a sports presenter on BBC Television and presented a regular BBC series, City Hospital.

His publicity material reads: "By combining his close understanding of motivation, the dynamics of teamwork and self-development with his personal experiences both on and off the track, he consistently inspires, motivates and entertains audiences throughout the country."

He was made an MBE in 1992.

Roger Black MBE

Olympic silver medallist Roger Black says he aims to give his audiences what they want. No clever stuff, just what the people come to hear.

And the message they expect from Roger is just how he overcame obstacles and achieved his goals. The glamour of the Olympic Games stirs their imaginations, of course, but essentially Roger stands up in front of them to motivate them.

Most of his motivational speaking is done at conferences, where his listeners usually take a more serious approach. After-dinner speaking with a gag a minute is not quite up his street. "That's a job for comedians," he says. "It's not what I do."

Part of the scene is that people want to know the thoughts and ideas of people who come from another world – in Roger's case, the world of international athletics – and they want to go away feeling they have had a great experience.

Too much store can be set by rubbing shoulders with a celebrity, says Roger. Most people are fascinated when they meet and talk to somebody who is a household name, maybe somebody they have seen on television, but that glitter soon fades, says Roger.

The motivational speech must therefore have substance, and Roger finds it rewarding when one of his audience buttonholes him after the speech and tells him: "I really enjoyed it." And this bouquet can come even from somebody who is not keen on sport.

Before he starts Roger reminds himself that his audience is often composed of people who have been at work all day, may not like sport anyway, and want a relaxing time, however serious-minded they are. He says you can tell when people are saying to themselves: "Oh, no, not another motivational speaker."

When he stands up to speak he realises he may have this kind of resistance to break down. Humour is the weapon to be used immediately. "Always start with a joke," he says. "Get them laughing within ten seconds. It makes them comfortable. Possibly indulge in a little self-deprecation. It goes a long way."

Then is the time to confirm to the audience exactly why he is there. The listeners have already been told but there is no harm in restating the case. Because the name of Roger Black is associated with athletic achievement he knows he has to take his listeners to the Olympic Games in their minds. The kind of success about which he enthuses is what motivates them but he is quick to point out: "They don't want to be bogged down with too much detail."

The enthusiasm is vitally important. Roger says: "If what you are saying comes from the heart it is real to them. And all I am doing is giving people my journey and my story. I can only give them the mindset of a champion."

Throughout his delivery he never forgets the way he started the speech. The people must continue to be amused, or their attention may be lost. "Keep them interested by mixing humour with the thought-provoking stuff," he says.

Even when the motivational speech is peppered with jokes and funny asides, people's minds can stray. They need a change of feel or a change of pace. Roger provides this with a video showing a few races. "It gives them a break," he says. "They need that if I am speaking for 40 or 45 minutes."

In Roger's strategy there are a couple of other pitfalls to avoid. "If you get too smart people will switch off," he warns. "And never bullshit. People will see through it."

People always like to have something memorable at the end of a speech and Roger has a couple of goodies up his sleeve. He shows them a video of the relay race at the 1991 World Championships. Britain won, so it's good patriotic material. Its other purpose is to emphasise the power of teamwork.

For the many who are interested, Roger brings along his medals, including the silver he won in the 400 metres at the 1996 Olympics. "People don't normally see these things," says Roger. Naturally, they often ask to hold the silver medal – it's that brush with fame again.

Roger also has a tip for speakers who address non-British audiences. Keep out the British references. Some speakers forget that Americans, for example, would not understand mentions of certain British comedians. Lack of understanding means a block on communication, and the speech will fall on its face.

Some people may ask why they need motivational speakers. Roger says: "You may make them think differently about something. Somebody may just want to hear what you are saying at that time."

Need a recap on Roger? Try this

- Start off with a laugh
- Tell them clearly what you are going to do for them
- Speak from the heart
- Keep them interested with some humour and visual aids to give the occasional change of pace
- Finish with something memorable

Richard Wilkins

Life has certainly been varied for the man who left school without any qualifications. Richard Wilkins's multi-faceted career began with training in plastering. It was not what he liked or wanted, partly because he despised the rip-off tactics he found in the trade.

He set up his own business in property development. Hard work earned him a mansion in Northamptonshire, with land that included the village green, and all the trappings of a wealthy lifestyle. He was in his thirties and was intending to retire at 40.

He had, however, borrowed heavily. When his wife left him he needed more borrowing, but the 1980s recession was biting and the bank called an abrupt halt. When the demand for repayment came Wilkins could not find the money and he became bankrupt.

At rock bottom and living in a bedsit, he worked for a while in a hospice. Then he borrowed £3,000 and produced his first book, a collection of sayings called *Ten Out of Ten – The Yellow Book*. It was the first of several, selling first in souvenir boutiques and later in mainstream bookshops.

The books supported him until he was asked to speak publicly. His inspirational addresses became his full-time occupation and he promotes his ideas on a catchily named website, www.theministryofinspiration.com. He now refers to himself as "an ex-millionaire who became a happy person."

Richard's interview

Dump all that theory. Even forget those pronouncements about positive thinking. Richard Wilkins speaks from the heart and offers himself as an example.

Wilkins calls himself an inspirational speaker, preferring the title to that of motivational speaker.

He says he never set out to be a public speaker. He went through a huge turnaround in his life, moving from wealth to bankruptcy and still managing eventually to come up smiling. His experience was such that people asked him to speak to audiences and the Wilkins bandwagon started to roll.

His message was that all people can feel good about themselves, which is how the idea of leading by example came in. Wilkins says he cannot be an example to his audience if he bowls in scruffily dressed. Nor can people take him seriously if he does not ooze that feeling of wellbeing.

The stage is set for Wilkins to tell his tale. He does not claim or want to lecture his listeners. He makes clear: "Really, I am a storyteller. People put on much bigger ears when you tell a real-life story."

The format of a story sits well with the Wilkins approach of going straight to the heart of the listener, not the mind. "Although my story is different from other people's my emotions are the same as theirs," he insists. "You must get there on an emotional level as well as an intellectual level."

He admits that this can be the difficult bit. The Brits have the same emotions as the rest of the world's people but are more reluctant to wear them on the sleeve. Wilkins has no problem with letting rip himself and just has to find a way of releasing his listeners' feelings. The audience often appears to be saying: "No emotions, please, we're British."

Wilkins usually breaks that ice with a good laugh. He has been known to tell people at the outset – quite truthfully – that he does not know what he is going to say. The people in their rows of seats giggle when he admits this. Just in case they don't believe him, he repeats that he has no idea what he will be saying.

Wilkins speaks as he feels and this means the story is different every time it is told. For this kind of performance there is no script.

Most times the Wilkins raw candour does break the ice, probably because it exposes his vulnerability and puts people at their ease. Once when facing an audience in Denmark he expressed his genuine fear that the language barrier would be a problem and that he would be misunderstood, or not understood at all. The honesty and the show of vulnerability worked again. He had tickled the heavy Nordic sense of humour and they all laughed. They understood English perfectly, of course.

Having got the audience on his side, Wilkins passes on his optimistic message by sharing his natural enthusiasm for living. "I believe we have only one ultimate goal and that is to feel good," he says. So he uses words and movement to spread that good feeling around his listeners.

It seems to come naturally, like his own feeling of wellbeing. He waves his arms and occasionally leaves the ground. He appears almost to dance in front of his audience. They smile and they laugh and the message comes across.

Having shared his love of life throughout his talk, Wilkins finishes on a high note. He informs the people that he feels incredible and promises to show them how incredible they are.

"I want you to imagine what the world would be like if everybody was like you," he tells them. It is a somewhat startling, even if morale-boosting, thing to say. They may feel a little surprised, but he goes on and asks: "Are there any muggers in the room? Any terrorists or any murderers?"

Of course there are not, and the people all loosen up again. "In this way I get them to realise they are doing much better than they thought," he says.

An earlier experience helped him to think this way. For a while he worked in a hospice, which most people would expect to be a gloomy place. Wilkins found the opposite. "People look back and realise how good their lives have been," he recalls. "And dying people don't bullshit."

Having broken through the emotions barrier and shared his enthusiasm, he hopes his listeners will leave feeling "uplifted".

His enthusiasm was born of hard experience. He boarded the commercial treadmill and made a fortune in his thirties. The recession and a broken marriage destroyed it all and he had to swap the 35-room mansion and the fast cars for an existence in a bedsit. He even contemplated suicide.

Then he realised the greatest thing he had lost was his self-worth and the rebuilding began. He has since appeared on television and has told his story on various shows, including the Kilroy and Esther Rantzen programmes.

His type of presentation must be going down well. After he appeared on The Last Word, which was compered by the comedian Les Dennis, he was asked by the production company whether he would like his own show.

How Wilkins puts the message across

- Be a living example of what you stand for
- Appeal to the emotions with a story, not an intellectual argument
- Make 'em laugh
- Share your enthusiasm
- Tell people everybody can be happy
- Send the audience away uplifted

Gerard O'Donovan

Gerard O'Donovan has developed a speciality of training life coaches through his company Noble Manhattan Coaching in Weymouth, Dorset. He has done it at a time – the end of the second millennium and the beginning of the third – when coaching and mentoring is becoming more and more in demand.

O'Donovan, born and raised in County Cork, entered his profession after experiencing several other fields. He was in the Royal Marines from 1975 to 1984 and went into insurance when he left the military.

After a spell in the insurance and financial worlds he set up a property business. However, the timing was wrong and he lost a lot of money in that market.

The tide was soon to turn. He set up his own financial services company in 1988 and eventually employed a staff of 1,000.

In 1992 he sold the company to the huge Cornhill insurance group and started Noble Manhattan, offering personal development services and now specialising in the training of life coaches.

Gerard's interview

It seems so simple when the motivational speaker takes the stage looking wonderfully confident.

Gerard O'Donovan puts us right. "A lot of people want to do motivational speaking," he says, "yet the ability to motivate others is a gift and it isn't as easy as you might imagine."

O'Donovan, who mixes his speciality of training life coaches with motivational speaking, warns the young hopefuls that the role is far removed from that of a stand-up comedian, however alike the two may seem from the auditorium.

"There is a big difference between the hot bath method and genuine motivational speaking," he says. "You feel great after a hot bath, but the sensation does not last. My job is to instil or embed what I say into my audience."

So what is the O'Donovan recipe? The first ingredient is essentially having wide experience. O'Donovan believes we all need to learn from others – and we all do. We learn from parents, teachers, work colleagues and many others. However, the key word is learning, not copying, because an imitation that achieves a near miss really disappoints and casts doubt on the speaker's sincerity.

"You must be yourself, not try to be anyone else," he says. The speaker who struggles to be an admired hero or heroine loses genuineness and credibility right away.

The second ingredient has to be commitment, which is similarly part of the genuineness. "You must be totally committed to giving value and being of service," says O'Donovan. After all, the people who come along to be motivated can usually sniff you out if you are not committed to your message.

The third ingredient follows naturally. The speaker must know the subject inside out, also to establish credibility. The homework is so important, believes O'Donovan. He advises: "We must embark on a process of learning ourselves and thus get better. It behoves all motivational speakers to upgrade themselves. For example, the 1980s and 1990s techniques are no longer acceptable."

He explains that a business audience would be frightened off by the aggressive tactics of the speakers of those two decades. The acceptable approach in the early part of the 21st century is a softer coaxing one.

Every speaker, while observing the general rules, has an individual style, of course. O'Donovan's performance is one that is on the move. He says: "I bring a huge amount of energy and movement to a presentation, and it can be contagious." He finds his lively performance first catches the attention of the audience and then gets people on his side. "Be genuinely enthusiastic and you can pass the enthusiasm on to others," he says.

So, learning from others, being committed and knowing your subject are O'Donovan's principles when he steps up on to the stage. However, there are some must-not-dos in his virtual manual.

It is essential, he says, that the speaker does not concentrate on his own oratorical skills. Nobody should be implying to the audience: "Just listen to my oratory." It would mean that the speaker has lost sight of the purpose of the speaking. Any skills from the platform should be vehicles to help the audience, not to impress them.

O'Donovan's other warning is to avoid trying to be Superman or Superwoman. The brash salesman may sound thrusting and powerful when he boasts that he sold all of £4 million worth of computers last year and then bawls out: "You can do it too." Most members of the audience will say under their breath: "No, I can't."

The result will be that the people whom the speaker is trying to court and persuade are intimidated and turned off.

Here we return to O'Donovan's axiom that he aims to instil or embed his message in his listener's minds. His vital message is that the answers lie within the men and women to whom he is speaking. Motivation means being the catalyst to bring out those answers. O'Donovan says: "You must help them to reach their own immense levels of resources. This is cognitive restructuring, or helping people to think in a different way."

Motivating people to dig deep to find their abilities for themselves seems to be something of a mission for O'Donovan. He says: "The reason why many people don't achieve something is that they don't realise they can or believe they can, and a good motivational speaker will get them to understand that. The motivator helps you to see the truth about yourself and free your own motivation."

He considers this is an honest approach but feels that many people cannot take such a step because they are influenced by, among other things, commercial advertising. The images thrust at them of actors and models with perfect physiques and folk with highly successful careers actually tear away their self-esteem, rather than inspiring them. They are the opposite of what he tries to get across to his listeners. He does not ask people to model themselves on celebrities or dynamic business people but to find and realise their own uniqueness and their own potential.

He also believes that too many people are also misled by popular sayings. Is ignorance really bliss? Certainly not, he says. What you don't know *can* hurt you.

Can the leopard not change his spots? "It's true for the leopard," says O'Donovan. "But people can change radically, and they can change in a heart beat. I believe that even the ones who don't change can change if they want to."

He ends up with the four Cs that his listeners should shun. He tells them not to Criticise or Condemn others and not to Complain all the time. Nor should they Compare themselves with the image idols. Instead they should "look within" and draw out all that valuable potential.

Gerard's tips

- Be yourself
- Do your homework
- Commit to your message
- Show enthusiasm
- Realise your own potential

Geoff Burch

Geoff Burch, born and raised in Cheltenham, Gloucestershire, got his academic piece of paper at an art college. However, he went into the advertising world after his qualification and started to earn a living from copy writing.

This led to selling, which he found "one of the most exciting things in the world." The reason was partly the humour that for him always accompanied a sales pitch.

Burch's business career took off first when he ran his own small group of companies but he sold out in the 1980s as the whole scene became "too worrying."

He followed this by setting up a marketing and management consultancy, which was more to his liking. It was at this time that he was approached by clients for training. "People asked me to change their employees," he says.

The training aspect of the job laid the foundations for what Burch now does. In his own words, he drifted into motivational speaking. He has since broadened his portfolio with after-dinner speaking.

To date he has set out his theories and views in three books – *Resistance is Useless, the Art of Business Persuasion*; *Go It Alone, the Streetwise Secret of Self-Employment*; and *Writing on the Wall*.

He still runs his business from Cheltenham.

Geoff's interview

Laughter. It's probably the oldest trick in the book for winning people over and it's an integral part of Geoff Burch's style for motivating an audience.

Burch is a rebel among motivational speakers. He looks down his nose at the hype of optimism and positive thinking that make up the vocabulary of most of his fellows. "I have a sideways view of things and take the mickey out of motivational speakers," he says.

But don't get the wrong idea. Burch does not reject the positive-minded approach. He just thinks that it is often used to cover up reality. His simplest illustration is of a speaker encouraging his listeners to make the journey from London to Sheffield. The pie-in-the-sky man paints a rosy picture of Sheffield and enthuses that you have to go there. Burch, on the other hand, would tell you how far away Sheffield is and what the pitfalls are, and then he would direct you to decide whether or not to go.

He says he gives people the reality of any situation before he can motivate them. "I am accused of being cynical," he says, "but what I do is to clarify the position as it really is."

Then there is the laughter technique. When it comes to inspiring an audience or an individual to take action, the motivation is mixed with humour. Burch amuses and informs at the same time. "Like all observational humorists I destroy bores by making them laugh," says Burch. "You can't resist somebody who makes you laugh."

He recalls one of his more unorthodox assignments. Instead of the usual eager executives and salespeople he confronted a roomful of dustmen and other council workers. They sat in rows with their arms folded just waiting for more monotonous garbage. An immediate joke softened them up. The Burch method of tickling their tonsils got them on side. He laughs too: "It worked like a virus."

Alongside laughter he uses the element of surprise — even shock. Burch is known for waking up an assembled audience by riding a large motorcycle through them and on to the stage. If nothing else, his noisy entrance captures people's attention.

This, however, is just one of a combination of tactics to gain the trust of an audience. Burch often arrives for the session on his motorcycle, but there is more incongruity. He wears a well-tailored three-piece suit and sports a ponytail. What do you make of that? The unusual mixture of mode of transport, executive dress and eccentric hair throws the audience off balance, gets them wondering what will happen next and makes them receptive.

Burch observes that people often judge others by their status and try to see where they themselves line up in the pecking order. However, the smartly dressed motorcyclist with a ponytail is not measurable in this way and is non-competitive as a result. "Thus," says Burch, "you make them feel unthreatened and non-critical before you put across the message."

He then has his own approach to the motivation message itself. He aims to encourage people to believe in themselves as who they are. The first move must not be to chivvy them into being something different or highly ambitious.

Burch does not even expect people to be full of beans all the time. "You don't have to have a bouncy sunny disposition to succeed," he says. In fact, he refers to himself as a "depressing git"! Anyway, he believes lugubrious people usually live life on a more even keel.

He goes back to the gathering of council dustmen for an example of good motivating speaking. Burch maintains that few of them would take pleasure in doing a job badly. His job was to help them to do their job to their satisfaction. Council employees are also at the sharp end of a big organisation, the ones who are buttonholed by the public with questions and complaints, and this experience too can have its rewards. Burch believes he has to motivate such people to represent their business effectively. It should please them to do so.

It follows that when people have been helped to understand what they actually want, and they want to reach for the stars, they can be motivated to do just that.

Burch has one little sideline in understanding the people who ask him for help. His father was a Viennese psychiatrist who came to Britain at the start of the Second World War, bringing with him a theory about fairy stories.

If you have a favourite fairy story it says a lot about your background, believes Burch. "You can bet that the woman whose favourite is the tale of Cinderella had very strict parents," he says. "You can be sure too that she had an aunt like Bet Lynch who bought her nail varnish and took her to a night club."

Now, that's original, and it chimes with what Burch's own website tells us about his meetings: "You could fill a room with a cross-section of people, from a part-time cleaner to the chief executive of an international company, and everybody would come away with new ideas."

Some motivational steps in the Burch repertoire

- Surprise your subjects to throw them off balance
- Amuse them to get them on your side
- Make them see themselves as they are
- Reveal to them that they are happier doing a job well
- Find out what they want and then guide them to achieve their goals
- Sometimes dig a little deeper and examine their backgrounds – the fairy story theory may help!

Brian Collett

Brian Collett, who co-operated with Jacqui Harper in producing this book, has spent a lifetime in journalism, listening to and interviewing a range of people, from the proverbial men in the street to prime ministers and national presidents.

In his early days as a reporter he recalls sitting through local council meetings in which the elected representatives of the people droned on in their monotones, dealing with such exciting subjects as road widening and stopped-up sewers.

He recalls attending a conference in more recent times at which half the speakers literally succeeded in persuading delegates to nod off. "We could have died in our sleep listening to some of them," he says.

Yet neither the mundane councillors nor the conference speechifiers needed to be so boring if they had attended to their presentation skills. Roads and drains are important and the message that something is happening in a community should be put across in an interesting and relevant way. The same applies to any conference. If the organisers think the subject merits a conference it is the speakers' duty to communicate their information and views to those who pay to attend.

Brian was learning this fact of public life subconsciously and unintentionally as he moved through a journalistic career – what he calls his "criminal record".

He began as the cliché reporter on a bicycle, riding up and down Welsh hills to gather news. He worked on other local and provincial newspapers, including the *Western Daily Press* in Bristol, where many a good journalist wept and gnashed his teeth but learnt the principles of the trade. His provincial newspaper journey ended with several editorships.

He spent nearly 12 vital, productive years on *The Times*, and around this time worked as a freelance on other national newspapers, including the red-top tabloids. He feels *The Times* widened his scope for what was to come. Life after *The Times* has been devoted mainly to freelance writing. Brian calls it a patchwork experience of business journalism, newsletter editing and ghost writing.

He comes back to presentation. He sees many lost opportunities for enlivening subjects from the platform or the dinner top table. "These are the days of communication, yet people seem to be less well informed than they were 30 years ago," says Brian.

Hence the need for good presentation skills and this book, showing how the experts do it properly.

About Crystal Business Training

Crystal Business Training uses television techniques to create conferences, seminars and training courses for large corporate clients.

In conferences, their reputation is for designing and delivering strategy conferences for global banks.

Crystal Business Training provides the only UK service dedicated to achieving more effective Off Site/Away Day Events.

The bespoke training courses for business leaders or sales teams deliver major improvements in presentation skills, media interviews, teambuilding and motivation.

The Crystal Business team come from three key areas: television, business training and event management. The combination of leading experts from these different fields has resulted in unique training events that consistently exceed the expectations of clients. Those clients include global banks, international corporations and top UK financial companies.

As Managing Director of Crystal Business Training, Jacqui Harper advises global financial companies on effective communication of strategy. She works with companies to design Off Sites that deliver better results for their business. She also shows business leaders, managers and sales teams how to get their message across at meetings, pitches and media interviews. Jacqui was previously a TV presenter for BBC News, Sky and GMTV.

As Director of Crystal Business Speakers Jacqui provides expert speakers at financial conferences. Visit www.crystalbusinessspeakers.com for further details.

More information about Jacqui's training company can be found at the following website address: www.crystalbusinesstraining.com or call 0870 774 6220.